THOMAS A HEINZ

FRANK LLOYD WRIGHT FIELD GUIDE

WEST VOL 3

A.D. ACADE

Front cover: Taliesin West, Scottsdale, Arizona

First published in Great Britain in 1999 by
ACADEMY EDITIONS

a division of
John Wiley & Sons Ltd
Baffins Lane
Chichester
West Sussex PO19 1UD

ISBN: 0-471-97747-0

Printed and bound in Singapore

■ Buildings designed by Frank Lloyd Wright still survive in thirty-five states of the U and in England (the Kaufmann Office of 1937, which was originally sited in Pittsburgh, now in the V&A Museum, London) and Japan (see pp124-34). These buildings outsic North America are now revered and well protected. One wishes that this were true of th US works. They number over four hundred, if one includes bridges, windmills, gate and fountains. The Field Guides divide these buildings up into groups of roughly equ

size according to area: Upper Great Lakes, MetroChicago, West and East. The latter two guides encompass areas outside of the continental US, such as Japan in the West volume and England in the East volume. Projects that were drawn up for clients with intended sites in Central America, the Middle East and the southern portion of Asia are also incorporated into this West Field Guide (see World Map p15), as Wright's practice was becoming an increasingly international one in the last two decades of his life.

■ This Field Guide is to Wright's building designs in the western half of the US, Hawaii, Western Canada, Mexico, Central America, Japan, the Middle East and Southern Asia.

At the back of the guide a geographical list of works first gives all sites and buildings within each state in the US alphabetically by city before citing the designs outside North America by country. A complete list of all of Wright's buildings is also included and is arranged alphabetically by the last name of the original client or, if it is a commercial structure, by the proper name of the building. When a building has an alternative, popular name this also appears. Buildings featured in this volume are identified by page number. Buildings featured in other volumes in the series are identified by volume.

The primary source for the maps is the United States Geological Survey, which issues detailed topographic maps for the entire United States.

Star Ratings

The rating system used throughout the book is based on the author's opinion, and takes into account several important factors: the extent to which Wright's design philosophy is expressed in the individual building; the current condition; the impact of later alterations; and the ease with which the building can be viewed. These factors give an overall rating to the property, and no area is weighted over another. This system thus gives some indication of the effort one should expend to visit a building.

Opus Numbers

The Director of Archives at the Frank Lloyd Wright Foundation, Bruce Brooks Pfeiffer, has assembled a list of all of Wright's buildings and projects and assigned a reference number to each, based on the year of the project and the chronology of projects within that year. While a few inaccuracies may appear, this has proved the best method of identifying individual designs. All drawings and photographs in the foundation's archives are identified with these numbers plus an added code for each individual drawing or photograph. Ideally, this system would be extended to include each piece of furniture and panel of art glass.

GPS Numbers

The Global Positioning System (GPS) has now been accepted as an accurate locational device used in sea and air travel. A series of time-keeping satellites send their time out to a receiver which calculates the difference in times between at least three of these satellites, giving a specific location and elevation. These GPS readings are accurate within a very narrow range. Soon automobiles, cellular telephones and portable computers will be fitted with these devices. GPS coordinates are included in this Field Guide as an aid to identifying locations.

C Numbers

These appear at the end of each building description. They note the date that the photographs were taken. The 'c' stands for circa.

Note to Readers

The publisher and author wish to reassert to the readers that the majority of these properties are privately owned and that the owners' legal rights should be respected accordingly. The publisher and author will accept no responsibility for any action taken against any readers who contravene this notice.

■ When Frank Lloyd Wright was born on 8 June 1867, there were only thirty-seven states in the Union – Washington, Wyoming and Oklahoma and several others were territories. (Arizona was the last state to join the continental US on 14 February 1912.) The territories were widely considered wilderness, and still large sections remain so. The wildness of 'the Wild, Wild West' was not limited to the untamed flora and fauna, but was also extended to some of the inhabitants. There were wild men and wild Indians. Even a staged event by Death Valley Scotty for the benefit of Albert M Johnson in the 1920s (see p41), where wild Indians 'attacked' them while traveling through the desert, was not too far fetched to be considered possible.

'Go west, young man!' remains as much a call to the adventurer as to the speculator. These days the call might be for 'plastics,' or more timely, 'computers.' Most of the clients who engaged Wright were born and raised in the East. What brought them west ranged from the flip of a coin in Chicago for Harvey Sutton (p89) to a new job such as becoming a beef inspector for Alexander Chandler (p83). Many clients were interested in cheap land and beautiful scenery, things that were not always possible in the more congested East. A third factor was the idea of easy wealth. The Gold Rush of the mid-nineteenth century brought streams of people west. There were also other 'waves,' which had the same effect: the land boom of 1889, the year Wright built his Oak Park home, proffered 40 acres to anyone who claimed it; and the discovery of oil in Texas and California, in the 1880s and through to the 1930s, worked as a magnet for many others. Others went west as an escape from the congestion and personal troubles that followed them. The climate of the West was reported to be good for one's health. The sunny and dry climate of Arizona and California still have that reputation. It was a chance at a new life. With the wide open spaces, people could get lost figuratively as well as literally. Wright went west twice. Once when he was trying to escape the taunts of his second wife, Miriam Noel, in 1927-28 and, later, when he was attempting to escape the cold, damp winter for his health while in his 60s.

Everywhere I have gone, nearly everyone has a Frank Lloyd Wright story. It might be about some building, or they may have met him; they may just have read something by or about him or his buildings. In researching for this series of books, I have found that the truth is stranger than fiction. The stories I have found are compelling and take many twists and turns. The directions that a simple project for a single family residence takes are often unexpected. For an architect, residential projects are usually considered to be near the bottom of the barrel, residential additions and remodelings being the scrapings. Yet, Wright certainly put everything he had into even the most modest of work. This might then be why his work has so much life in it, nothing was below him. No project was too small or insignificant. Wright put his full effort into every idea. Luckily, the best times in his life were for the most part also those of the greatest tranquillity. The time he spent with his third wife, Olgivanna Lazovich Hinzenberg (married August 1928), was perhaps the most tranquil. She helped him in much of the administration of the growing group of people that assisted in the development of his designs.

■ The first buildings Wright designed in the western region covered by this guide were at the end of what has been referred to as his first golden age, between 1900 and 1910, when he built his Prairie Houses in Oak Park, Chicago (see MetroChicago volume). His initial designs for the western US were for small houses. The first was executed in 1908 for Dr George Stockman for a little boom town in Central Iowa, Mason City (p105). A year later Wright carried out his second western design for a George Stewart, who built it in Montecito, near Santa Barbara, California (p44). In 1909, Como Orchards of Montana (p66) was also well on its way to becoming a sizable project, though there is no evidence that Wright supervized any of the buildings' construction in the town. The City National Bank and Hotel also for Mason City (p104) came soon after the Stockman House. Nothing else of note, however, was produced for the western area covered by this guide until the Imperial Hotel in Tokyo (pp129-31), and other buildings for Japanese clients in the late teens. In the 1920s, Wright's works in both California and Arizona, while not great in number, blossomed with ideas.

Wright's most varied work can be found among the sites and solutions for this part of the world. This might be a reflection of the sort of clients he was designing for and their apparent openness to experimentation. His creativity penetrated into every aspect of a job. The engineering that went into the Imperial Hotel remains among the most innovative earthquake solutions. This building was also one of the most highly decorated. It was one of the few, and certainly one of the largest, buildings where everything was designed by Wright: the furniture, dinnerware, rugs, light fixtures, as well as the sculpture and graphics. The abstract sculpture and the terra-cotta air-vent covers are fully integrated in scale and color.

The largest planning schemes were designed for the West. They spanned from the first decade of the century, when Wright designed Como Orchards in Montana, through to the 1940s when he planned the Hunting Hartford Resort (p51) for the Los Angeles area.

Some of the strangest looking designs for buildings are from this region. The Johnson Desert Compound Buildings for Death Valley (p41) are church-like in appearance and the Huntington Hartford Resort (p51) looks like a set of space ships.

The 1930s brought another new look to Wright's work with the Bazett and Hanna Houses (pp32-33). Wright broke the rigidity of the box-like volumes by eliminating their square corners through the use of a grid of hexagons instead of squares and rectangles. This allowed for spatial extensions in three dimensions.

Growing fame brought commissions for Central America, South Asia and the Middle East – India and Iraq respectively. While most of these buildings were to be houses, the schemes for the public buildings in Baghdad (p136) were outgrowths of Wright's search for more challenging geometries – the circle and its arcs and curves were explored in these projects.

The people behind the West designs are as individual and unique as the buildings that reflect them. Many of the clients have become well known names, others, while important, have faded into history. Like those who commissioned buildings from Wright elsewhere, the clients are interconnected through a network that is independent of their common denominator, that of being a Wright client. Many knew each other through their appreciation of fine art, others through business and still others were different generations of the same family. The McArthur brothers, for instance, who built the Arizona Biltmore Hotel (p74) were the sons of a Chicago client Warren McArthur (see MetroChicago volume).

As pioneers who traveled west in the twenties from the Midwest, seeking new opportunities, the McArthurs were among Wrights most important western clients. They created a continuum with his clients of the teens and early twenties, most prominent of which were his California patrons, such as Aline Barnsdall (p56) and Alice Millard (p61). They also became a conduit for a new class of clients, who knew the Biltmore, and wanted a hotel of their own, such as: Alexander Chandler who commissioned San Marcos in the Desert in 1928, the year following the design of the McArthurs' hotel, in Chandler, Arizona (p83); and George Huntington Hartford II who was behind the Huntington Hartford Resort of 1947 in Beverly Hills.

The later clients were greater in number, as they came to Wright once his fame had spread through popular magazines and newspaper articles, and his own public presentations and appearances. Publicity in the last couple of decades thus became an important link in the expansion of his practice.

Wright's own family figured in his work in the West not only through the house he built for his son David (p80), but also through his long association with his eldest son, Lloyd, who remained a Los Angeles architect.

Wright never seemed to be bothered by 'the ones that got away.' With 80 percent of an architect's work completed at the conclusion of the drawing phase, these designs are as important to an architectural practice as those that are built. The unbuilt projects go unbuilt for a myriad of reasons, only some of them economic. The Rogers Lacy Hotel (p99) projected for Dallas is a very good example: Mr Lacy died just before construction began. The newspapers speculated whether or not his heirs would build the design with the money from his estate, which was many times greater than the cost of the hotel. They did not. Economics were, however, often decisive. The stock market crash of 1929 affected the work on two other hotels: the San Marcos in the Desert and the already standing Arizona Biltmore; construction of the San Marcos was halted and the Arizona Biltmore ran into financial difficulties.

Only sixteen non-residential buildings in this region were realized. The remaining structures were all single family residences. This ratio seems quite high. Many of his greatest engineering feats were conceived to be located in this region from the built Imperial Hotel to the San Marcos and Biltmore block projects, and the butterfly bridge for San Francisco Bay (p29) to the Hanna and Griggs Houses (pp33 and 19 respectively), all contained advanced innovative engineering concepts that seem daring even today.

Use your imagination to conjure up the San Marcos in the Desert, Doheny Ranch (p52), Lake Tahoe Summer Colony (p38), Morris House (p28), Rogers Lacy Hotel and Lenkurt Electric Company (p31) in their settings – these few schemes alone make Wright stand apart from all other architects. Add to this that they all came from a man who was over sixty years old, and one can see why Wright's work needs to be looked into and better absorbed for its potential ideas and directions by those of us working today.

It is, however, Taliesin West that perhaps provides the most vital key to Wright's particular attunement and orientation to the West in his later years. From 1938 onwards, the entire Taliesin Fellowship – students, apprentices, architects, spouses and staff – moved each fall to the encampment in Arizona via automobile caravan, only to return to Taliesin, Wisconsin, in the spring. During the journeys across America, there were side trips to National Parks, the homes of clients and major cities to visit museums or the opera. Though this seasonal move was initially done largely for the sake of Wright's health, Taliesin West also provided him with a winter base for meeting clients (many of the descriptions in this Field Guide mention how the clients were invited out to Arizona), and a particular context for them and the public to see him in.

Taliesin West in the forties and fifties still epitomized the extremity of the West and its frontier landscape. Situated at the base of the McDowell Mountains, in what is now northeast Scottsdale, near Phoenix, it had an unyielding desert setting. The dramatic scenery not only gave it a sense of man's smallness and fragility in comparision to nature, but also had an ancient Native American inheritance – it was once occupied or at least used by the Hohokam, something of which Wright was fully aware as there were archaeological excavations in the vicinity during his lifetime.

Wright's association with Taliesin West, and its closeness to Native American culture, helped to formulate for him both the concerns and the image of the uniquely American architect who was sensitive to the site specific and the climatic in architecture. The natural setting of Taliesin West was integral to his own perception of it. He wrote to Fowler McCormick, a neighbor and major landowner in Scottsdale in 1949, 'You are perfectly right in feeling the primitive in Taliesin West. In the ancient days of the race men were close to nature as a child to its mother.' Hot during the day and cold at night with very little rainfall, Arizona invited Wright to make very different solutions for housing to those he worked on in the East and the Great Lakes, which had to be effective in freezing temperatures and snow, as well as fully waterproof. It also secured a modern tradition for working in this mode – the Taliesin Fellowship eventually made Taliesin West its permanent base and the Frank Lloyd School of Architecture is now located there. Today, it is contemporary architects of the Southwest – the likes of Will Bruder, Wendell Burnette and Antoine Predock – with direct and indirect connections to the school or the fellowship, rather than those of the East, who are most visibly working in an innovative Wrightian vein.

Now Taliesin West has a very different feel to it from even twenty years ago, though the buildings are still there. Back then, it felt boundless. Only the rise of the valley into the McDowell mountains contained it. To the east, west and south, it was limitless as was the desert. In contrast, today, it is constricted by the Hayden Rhodes Aqueduct. The electrical high-tension wires and the encroaching spread of housing developments are taking away the desert and adding so much water to the air that it is trapping the pollution that this type of development brings with it. The walls that keep the residents secure makes one feel as though one is driving down the bottom of a gulch on many of the main roads around Taliesin West. The sign 'To Taliesin' has also gone. It is not so much a nostalgic longing for something that was once there as a need for historical accuracy, in order to understand what Wright created, that is important. It is not necessary to have his work interpreted, if it can be received straight from him through the experience of his buildings and their intended settings.

If Wright's awareness of the specific qualities of a house's site was heightened by his relationship with Taliesin West, it is apparent right the way through his buildings for the West. Many of their locations are unusual and they distinguish themselves from those of the East and the Upper Great Lakes through their special sense of place. This is immediately apparent when visiting a house, such as the Millard House in Pasadena (p61), where its particular position and view on its valley makes it appear as if it belongs to a different location to that of the rest of the neighborhood. A similar acute sensitivity to site is at play in many of Wright's other houses, most notably the Pearce House (p62), Hanna House (p33) and Gordon House (p20).

One of the surprises encountered on visiting many of the buildings in the west of the United States is that many of them are obscured by plants. These plants do not lose their leaves in the winter like those in the Midwest. There is therefore 'no good time of year' to visit so that more of the building is revealed.

While maintenance of buildings in the Midwest and East have to be upheld to deal with ice, snow and rain, the western alternatives are often more destructive – earthquakes and mud slides in California. Many of the California buildings have had some major earthquake damage in the past several years. The Barnsdall House was closed for a time. Large pieces of the wall of the Ennis House (p55) are missing and the Hanna House is in a serious state of disrepair.

In all, the West volume contains some of Frank Lloyd Wright's most dramatic sites and most unusual buildings. The only way to really understand this work is to see it in person. Please take advantage of the opportunity.

The Imperial Hotel, Tokyo, under construction. Completed 1923.

■ Crossing the Mississippi River was a major step for early travelers and it was equally significant for Wright. His first buildings in the west of the United States were built in the second decade of his career for Nebraska and one for California. Now only six of the twenty-one west states do not have at least one example of Wright's work. Most of the buildings are widely separated by hundreds of miles. This contrasts greatly with the high concentration of Wright buildings in Oak Park and River Forest (see MetroChicago volume).

Just as the West represented the pioneer spirit within the United States, and for Wright, the moment at which he left the comfort and knowledge of his Midwestern roots, Wright's

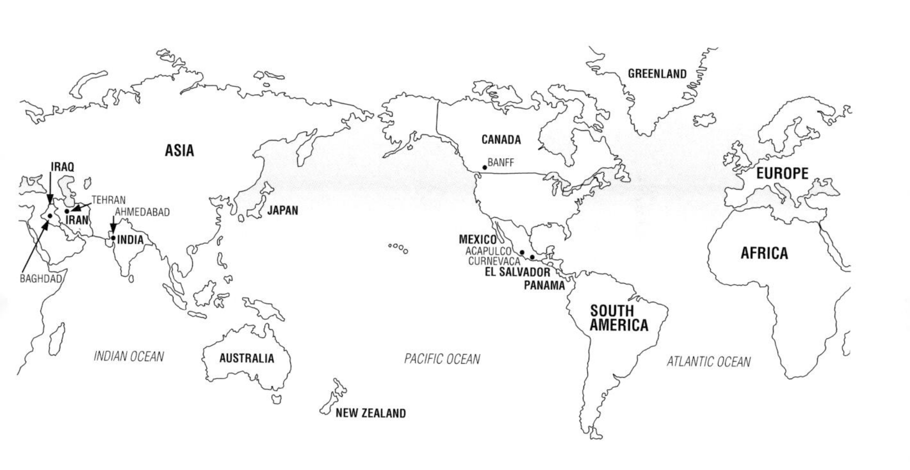

designs for those regions west of North America – Japan, Mexico, Central America, the Middle East and Southern Asia – epitomize his sense of exploration and experimentation, and his curiosity about other cultures. His work in Japan (pp124-34) between 1918 and 1923, in particular, was part of a longstanding romance with a foreign civilization's art and society. Though some of these projects would fit into cities almost anywhere in the world, the Baghdad projects of 1957 (p136), executed for the King of Iraq, are quite fantastic. While buildable, they conjure up a realm of genies, magic carpets and Middle Eastern tales.

SEATTLE AND PORTLAND AREA MAPS

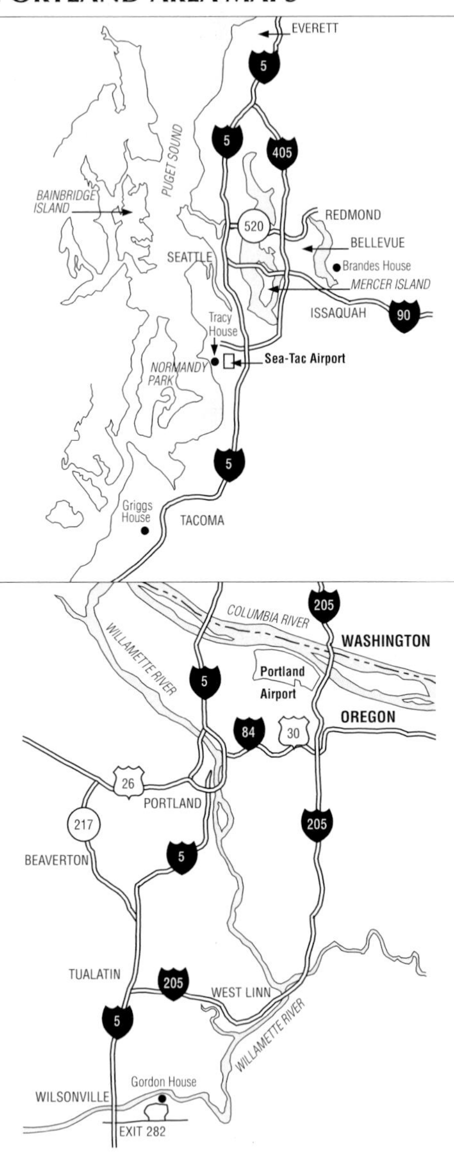

■ None of these houses can be seen without prior arrangement with the owners since they are all at a great distance from public roads. Most of them have been open on special tours in the last few years. The rainy weather in Seattle and Portland keeps the airborne dust to a minimum and makes everything appear to be very clean. Maintaining the roofs and flashings, however, is of utmost importance. The four buildings in the Seattle and Portland areas are constructed out of concrete block.

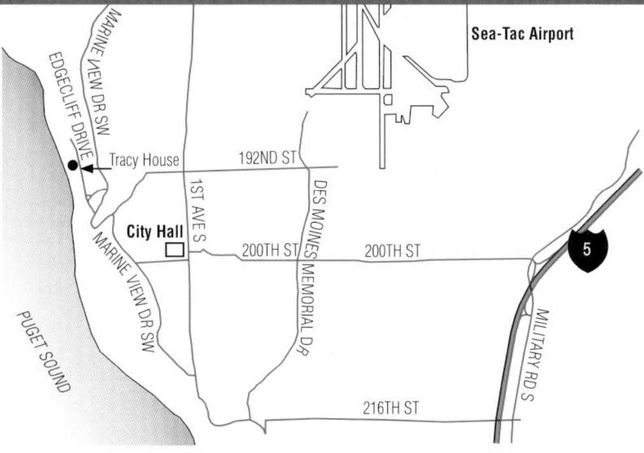

WILLIAM B TRACY HOUSE
18971 Edgecliff Dr,
SW Normandy Park,
Washington 98166
1954 5512

GPS: N 47 25.903
W 122 20.971

Directions: Exit Interstate 5, southbound at 200th Street and northbound at 200th Street/Military Road. Drive 2.5 miles past the Normandy City Hall to the dead-end at Marine View Drive Southwest. Turn north and drive through the S-turn on Marine View Drive to the Y-intersection taking the west branch onto Edgecliffe Drive and continue about one block to the address.

Accessibility: Only the front wall of the house can be seen from the street.

■ William Tracy began working for Boeing Aircraft in 1952. His wife, Elizabeth Tracy, knew of Wright's work having been taught by Goetsch and Winkler (see UGL volume) and Erling Brauner at Michigan State College. In 1954, Seattle architect Milton Stricker suggested writing to Wright for a house design with his endorsement. In March 1955, he received a good set of working drawings for their Usonian Automatic from Taliesin and hired Ray Z Brandes from nearby Issaquah (p18) as prime contractor. Prior to building starting in the early summer of 1956, the Tracys spent a year hand manufacturing the 1,700 blocks from metal molds. The $25,000 house was finished by August 1956. c94

RAY Z BRANDES HOUSE
2202 212th Avenue,
SE Issaquah
Washington 98027
1952 5204

GPS: N 47 35.418
W 122 03.235

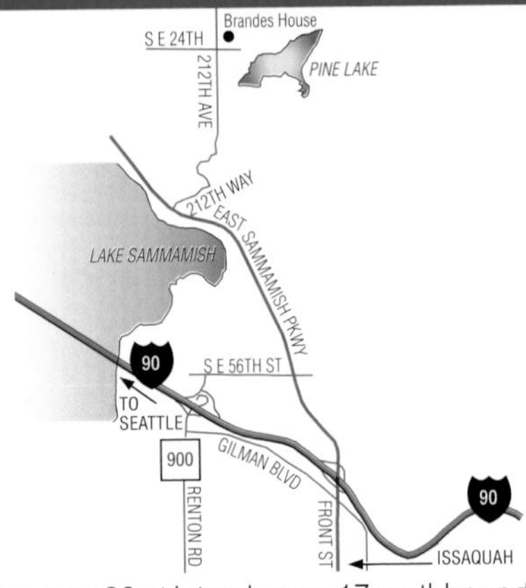

Directions: Issaquah is east of Seattle . Exit Interstate 90 at interchange 17 northbound onto East Lake Sammamish Parkway northeast for a mile to 212 Way Southeast. Drive through the curves past 24th Street. The driveway is north of Southeast 24th Street.

Accessibility: The house is down a long secured driveway .

■ Ray Brandes and his wife, Mimi (1905-64), sustained their family with home grown produce. Having started out as a photographer, he became a builder. (In 1956, he was the contractor for the Tracy House, p17.) He built four houses before he constructed his own on the 20-acre plot on the Sammamish Plateau. When the Brandeses wrote to Wright on 10 September 1951, they had a response within five days. On 15 November 1952, Brandes received the working drawings for a 1,950-square-foot house. By Christmas 1953, the family had moved in. The house is now lived in by Brandes's step daughter-in-law and her family. Brandes has moved to Arizona. c94

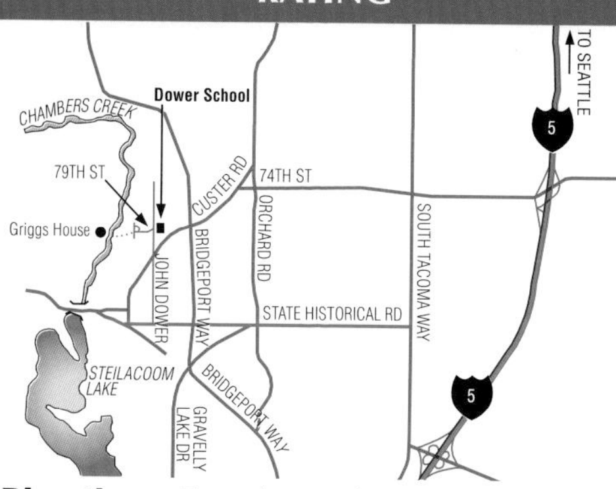

CHAUNCEY L GRIGGS HOUSE

6816 79th Street
W Tacoma
Washington 98467
1946 4604

GPS: N 47 11.142
W 122 31.657

Directions: From the north, exit Interstate 5 at 74th Street westbound. Drive for 2.2 miles and carry on where it turns southwest and changes its name to Custer Road for an additional 1.5 miles to John Dower Road. Turn north for 0.2 miles to 79th Street across from the Dower School. Turn west onto 79th Street for 0.2 miles to the end. The drive is to the south down the hill. From the south, exit Interstate 5 at interchange 125, Bridgeport Way northbound for 2.3 miles where it turns north and intersects Steilacoom Boulevard and turn west for 0.3 miles to John Dower and turn north, crossing Custer to 79th Street.

Accessibility: The house is down a very long drive and cannot be seen.

■ After graduating from Yale, Chauncey Griggs (1909-89) owned a successful lumber mill business. The design dates from 17 April 1946, but was not built until October 1954. Originally designed to have a waste-log roof, it was built with 1 by 12 cedar boards. c96

In 1919, Wright drew up a town plan for nearby Wenatchee. He probably gained this commission from RW Ludington, who lived in the town, previously a client in Dwight, Illinois (Opus #0616), and a partner of Smith (Opus #0410 and #0512).

CONRAD E GORDON HOUSE
7303 SW Gordon Lane
Wilsonville, Oregon 97070
1957 5710

GPS: N 45 17.645
W 122 45.261

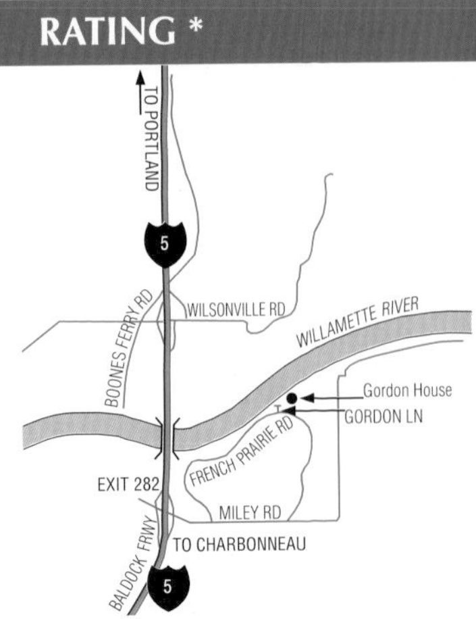

Directions: Wilsonville is south of Portland. Exit Interstate 5 at exit 282 eastbound on Miley Road for 0.2 miles or 0.7 miles and turn north onto French Prairie Road, a circular street that begins and ends at Miley Road. Follow French Prairie around to the little court across from Old Farm Road and turn north. The drive is to the east of the rear court.

Accessibility: On the Willamette River, the house is down a long drive.

■ Since marrying in the late 1920s, Myrtle Evelyn Gordon (1908-97) wanted a Wright house. Conrad Gordon drove stage coaches and did casual work, before starting up a dairy business. He went on, however, to become a member of San Francisco's prestigious 'Bohemian Club.' He owned a 250-acre property that included – before its removal to Aurora in the 1960s – an 1830s log cabin, part of the utopian Aurora Colony. Gordon contacted both William Wilson Wurster and RM Schindler, before writing to Wright on 3 March 1946. He waited to retire to construct the 2,200-square-foot house in 1963-64. c96

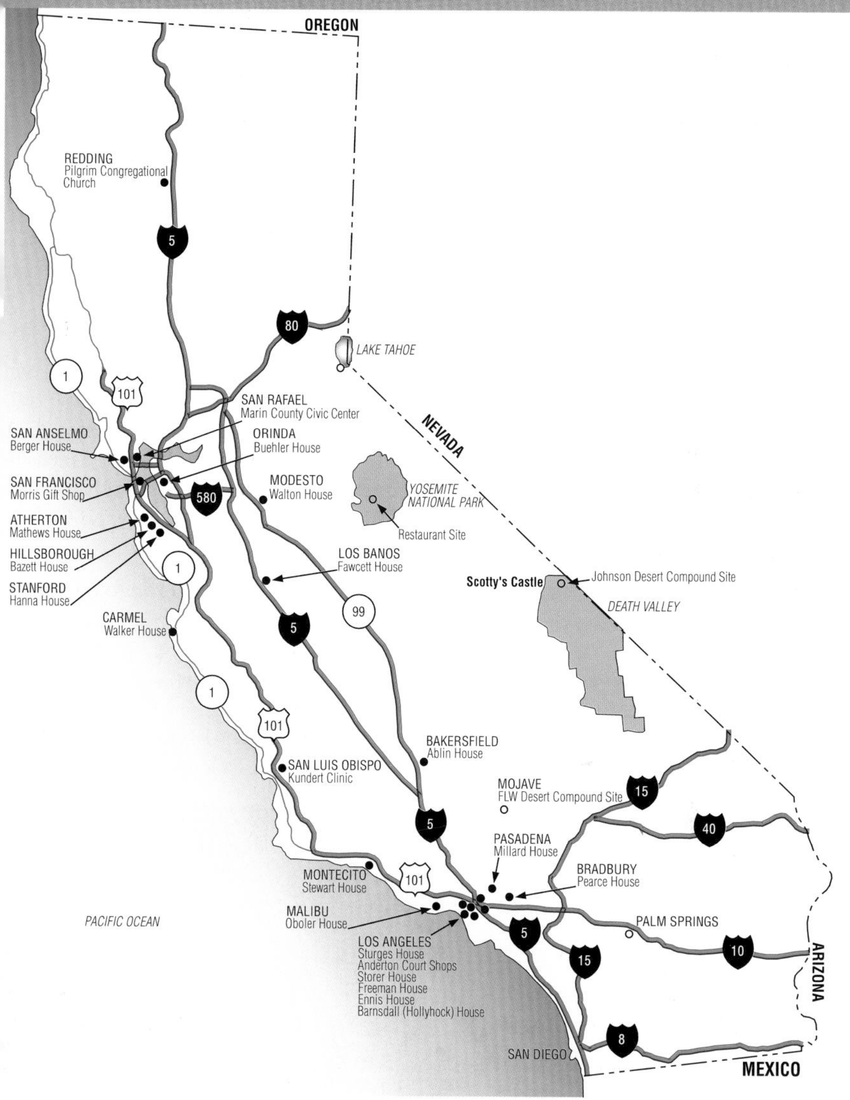

■ California has the largest population of any state in the US. It also has the greatest variety of geographic and geological features and climates. Though built work is widely dispersed, the most accessible buildings are in the cities with the two largest concentrations, San Francisco and Los Angeles. The buildings outside these urban areas are not lesser works, but are difficult to see without the owners' permission. It is worth noting that there are no buildings or projects in the San Diego–La Jolla area. As famous as Wright was, and despite Hollywood connections – his granddaughter was actress Anne Baxter – he also did not design any movie stars' homes.

PILGRIM CONGREGATIONAL CHURCH
2850 Foothill Boulevard
Redding, California 96001
1959 5818

GPS: N 40 35.021
W 122 24.750

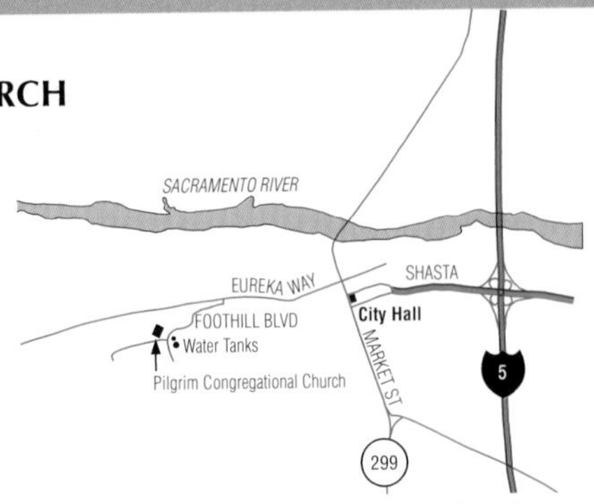

Directions: Exit Interstate 5 at Route 299 westbound and drive into the middle of town on Eureka Way for 1.3 miles. The street grid is a bit offset through town, about 5 or 6 blocks. Stay on Eureka Way for a mile past the downtown area to Almond Avenue. Turn about 300 feet south and turn west onto Foothill Boulevard and up the hill for 0.3 miles to the church across from Foothill Park and the concrete water tanks. The church is on the north side of the street, slightly below street level.

Accessibility: The church can be seen from the street and the parking lot.

■ The church was built for Reverend Ray L Wells who had a popular radio program in San Francisco. Preliminary drawings were completed in September 1959 and ground was broken in June 1960. Wright called this a 'pole and boulder Gothic.' Taliesin's Tony Putnam supervised the construction and the contractor for the first phase was Robert S Bryant. Dedicated in March 1963, the church is an unusual structure. The roof frames arch over the enclosure and are set at diagonals to the centerline of the sanctuary. Both the church and the adjoining schoolrooms are set low on the 5-acre site. c96

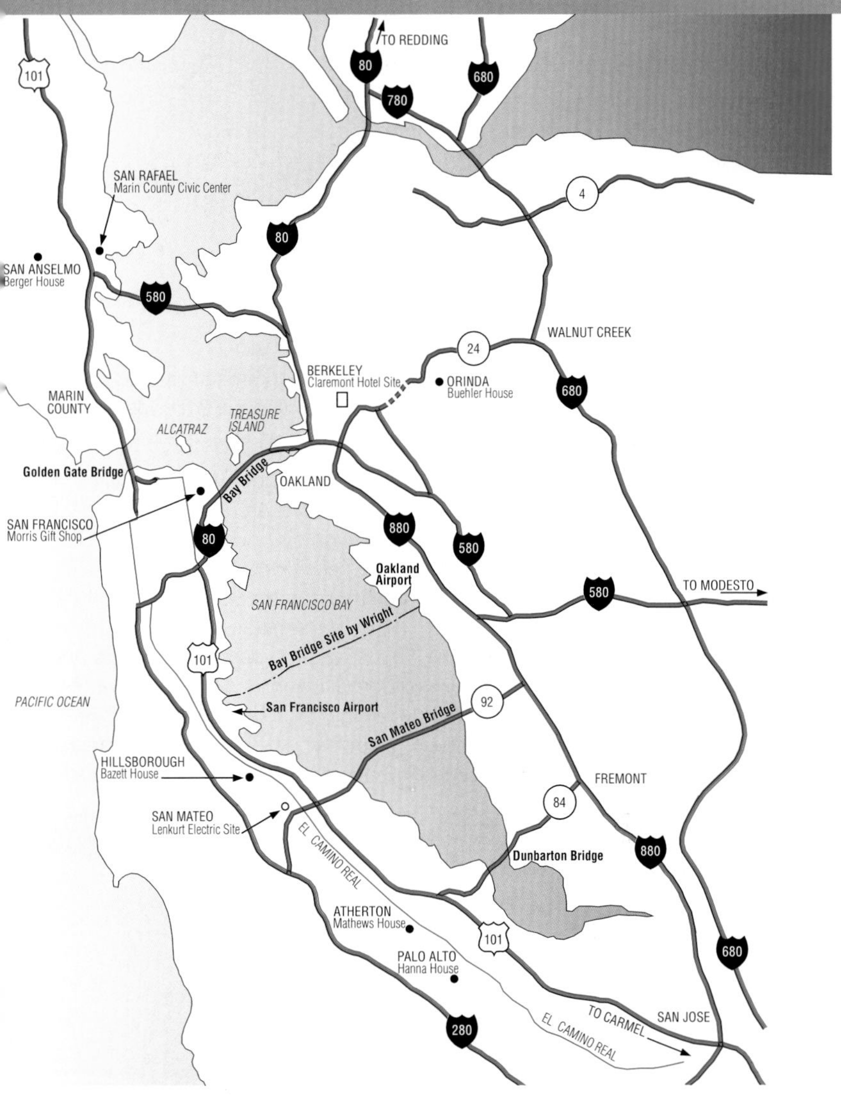

San Francisco Bay provides some of the most beautiful views in California. Its natural harbors were used by some of the earliest civilizations in the area. It also has one of the largest concentrations of Wright buildings. Some of the most interesting projects remain unbuilt, but if you visit the proposed sites it is easy to imagine the intended effect of the designs. This is particularly true of the Claremont Hotel's Wedding Chapel and the houses proposed for Morris on the coast (p28), west of the Golden Gate Bridge's cliffs. It also would be interesting to know how the Lenkurt Electric Company Building (p31) would have held up during the most recent earthquakes.

ROBERT BERGER HOUSE
259 Redwood Road
San Anselmo, California 94960
1950 5039

GPS: N 37 58.535
W 122 34.468

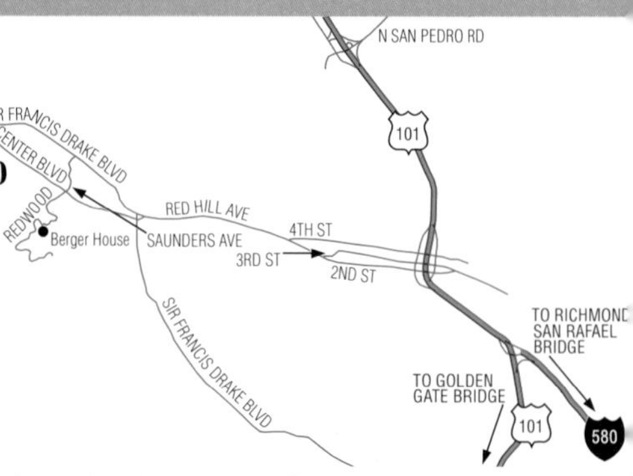

Directions: Exit US 101 at 3rd westbound and pass over Sir Francis Drake Boulevarc to Center Boulevard. Turn off left at Redwood Road and continue 0.5 miles to the house

Accessibility: The house can be seen from the street.

■ An engineering professor at the College of Marin, Robert Berger initially tried tc design his own house in a Cape Cod style. After reading *Architectural Forum* in 1948 however, he decided that he wanted Wright to design his house. He wrote to Wright ir 1950 with a list of some twenty-two requirements. These included producing a scheme that would be easy for him to build and accommodating radio equipment. When the plans arrived in 1951, Berger was serving in the Korean War. In 1954 Berger workec nights, constructing the house during the day. After two years, the Bergers and thei four children moved into phase one: the living room, kitchen, a bathroom and a bedroom A bedroom and and playroom wing was added in the second phase. Phase three, whict began in 1959, included a workshop and garage. Berger did all the work himself includin making the furniture. The Bergers met Wright once, but he never visited the house. c94

MARIN COUNTY CIVIC CENTER

North San Pedro Road
San Rafael, California 94903
1957 5746, 5754, 5755, 5756, 5757

GPS: N 37 59.818
W 122 31.684

Directions: The center is north of the Golden Gate Bridge east of US 101. Exit US 101 at North San Pedro and drive east for 0.25 miles to the center.

Accessibility: The building is open during business hours. It is visible on all sides from the street.

■ In June 1957, the County of Marin officially selected Wright to be the architect of the civic center. In July, he gave a personal address to the people of the county. By March 1958, he had submitted the center's plans. In November 1959, final plans were approved, and the contractor Rothschild, Raffin & Weirick, Inc was confirmed.

A 160-acre site with several tall and steep hills is not an obvious choice for a 4-story office building. It has, however, been used to the full to make one of the most spectacular solutions for a large-scale office and administrative center. This is in spite of a large area given over to car parking. The densely planted trees in the parking lot lessen the visual impact of the cars and afford some shade from the hot sun. The 14-acre lagoon has a 2-acre island, which provides a natural habitat for birds and plants.

On site there are also four theaters: three indoor and one outdoor, and a portable auditorium. The 500-foot-long south wing, which accommodates the Administration Building was the first to be completed. Its 172-foot-tall tower, which houses one of the main exhausts, supports the flag pole. Construction commenced in January 1960 and the center was dedicated in October 1962. Unlike most of today's civic structures, the construction change orders comprised only 1 percent of the total construction costs. The south wing construction cost less than $23 per square foot to build. In contrast with the Price Tower, built in the same year, at a reported cost of over $60 per square foot, it was a very economical building. The Hall of Justice was built next and was occupied by December 1969. Across the lagoon to the north is the 22,500-square-foot Exhibition Pavilion. The fairgrounds occupy about 80 acres and include the Marin County Fair in its schedule. The Marin County Civic Center is by far the largest building ever built to Wright's design. c77

The post office opposite the civic center (Opus #5753) was designed in tandem with the center's Administration Building. Plans were drawn up in 1957 and it was completed in May 1962. A football-shaped building in plan, it is similar in shape and scale to the house for Wright's son, Robert Llewellyn, in Bethesda, Maryland (Opus #5312). The elevations, however, are not nearly as interesting. It is the only federal building Wright designed. It was built on land leased from the county. c82

■ The rigid grid system of San Francisco, offset along Market Street, makes no allowances for its very hilly and beautiful site. Its famous Russian, Nob and Telegraph Hills are not apparent on the gridded map. This is one of the best cities to walk around. The streets are a bit narrower than those of most big cities, which adds to rather than detracts from the pedestrian scale. The Morris Gift Shop (p29), for instance, is located on a former alley. You can also take the commuter trains, BART, to the Wright sites and buildings at Berkeley (p29) and Stanford (pp33-35).

VC MORRIS GIFT SHOP
140 Maiden Lane
San Francisco, California 94108
1948 4824

GPS: N 37 47.031
W 122 24.283

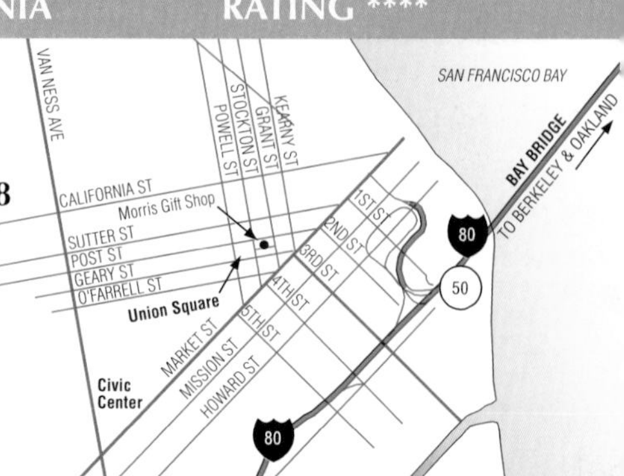

Directions: Exit Interstate 80 at 3rd Street and drive west four blocks until it becomes Kearny Street, continue two blocks to Sutter Street. Turn west onto Sutter Street for two blocks to Stockton Street. Drive south two blocks on Stockton to Union Square. Maiden Lane is at the center of the east block of the square. The shop is on the north side of the block about half way between Stockton and Grant. Watch out for one-way streets.

Accessibility: The building can be seen from the street.

■ Before he moved to San Francisco, Vere Chase Morris taught at the Parsons School of Design in Manhattan. He met Wright at a talk Wright gave in Palo Alto. The gift shop is a remodeling of an older warehouse. The original structure can be seen through the circular ceiling panels. Wright first produced a design for a house for Morris in 1945 (Opus #4303) for a site west of the Golden Gate Bridge. He executed a larger design for the same site in 1955 (Opus #5412), with a guest house (Opus #5530). When Morris died in 1957, Wright designed 'Quietwater' for his widow, on a flat site at Stinson Beach (Opus #5729). She, however, passed away before the working drawings were completed. c75

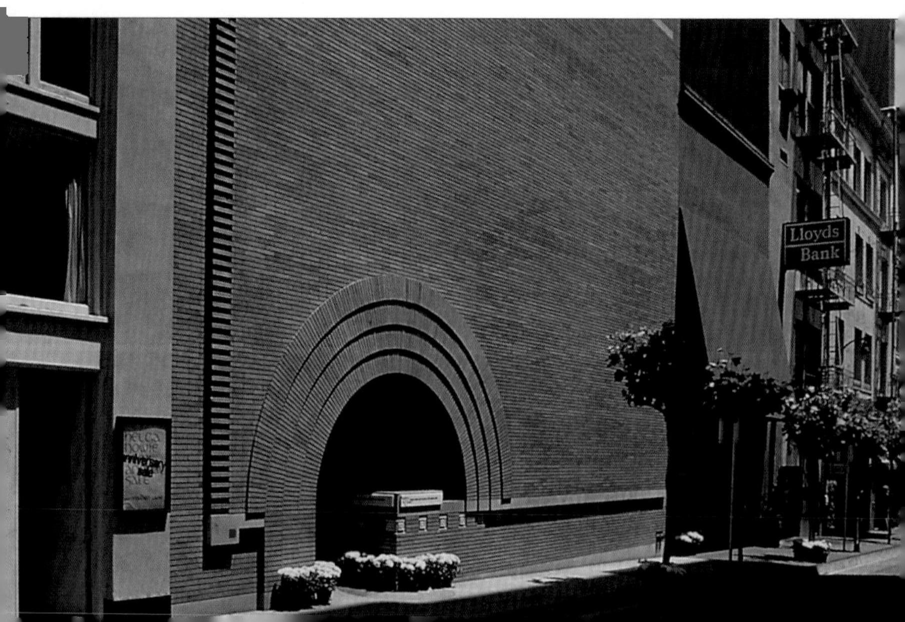

SAN FRANCISCO BAY AREA SITES

See maps on pp23 and 27 for locations.

SAN FRANCISCO BAY BRIDGE SITE
1949 4921

■ This bridge would have spanned San Bruno on the west and San Leandro on the east. It was to be a beautiful assembly of concrete arches with a small green area in the center. Its construction was opposed by the Sierra Club who claimed that it would impair the view and the BART train system was sufficient for commuters' needs.

SAN FRANCISCO CALL BUILDING SITE, corner of 3rd and Market Streets
1912 1207

■ This building was proposed for *The San Francisco Call*, the earliest paper in the city. Established in 1855, it was purchased by John D Spreckels (1853-1926), 'the Sugar King,' in 1895, and was sold in 1913 to William Randolph Hearst. Wright's son John Lloyd Wright's employer, Harrison Albright (1866-1933), probably put Wright forward for the job.

DAPHNE FUNERAL HOME SITE, 1 Church Street
1945 4823

■ Nicholas Daphne's funeral business was, in part, the model for the one in Evelyn Waugh's novel *The Loved One*. The intended site at Church Street was one of the finest lots in the city. Wright also designed a house for Daphne in San Mateo (Opus #4830). The Wright designs were not built because he felt that neither of them was workable. Born in 1908, in Greece, Daphne died in 1990. The current structure was designed by A Quincy Jones and is threatened with demolition.

AARON GREEN/FRANK LLOYD WRIGHT OFFICE SITE, 319 Grant Street
1952 5226

■ This is the original location of the Green/Wright office interior. Initially occupied by Taliesin apprentice Fred Langhorst (1905-79) between 1942 and 1950, the interior was redesigned and rebuilt by Green with the aid of an assistant, with the approval of Wright. Born in Florence, Alabama, Green acted as an intermediary for Wright's clients, the Rosenbaums (Opus #3903). He was a Taliesin apprentice until he entered the army in 1943. In 1988, Green dismantled the interior and sold it to the National Center for the Study of Frank Lloyd Wright. It was later acquired by the Heinz Gallery in Pittsburgh and installed in the Carnegie Museum there (see East volume).

WEDDING CHAPEL SITE, Claremont Hotel, Berkeley
1957 5709, 5731

■ This wedding chapel was designed for the hotel garden to seat about eighty people and cost about $50,000. Murray Lehr was Wright's contact at the hotel. Though he requested that it be completed by 1 April 1957, working drawings were not received until July 1957.

MAYNARD P BUEHLER HOUSE
6 Great Oak Circle
Orinda, California 94563
1948 4805

GPS: N 37 51 787
W 122 10.117

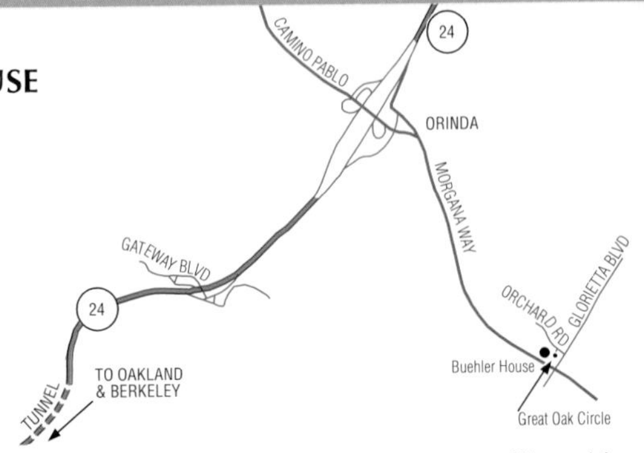

Directions: Orinda is to the east of Berkeley. Exit Route 24 at Morgana Way, drive southbound for 1.6 miles to the traffic lights at Glorietta Boulevard. Drive east about 250 feet up Glorietta and take the left turning that is Orchard Road. Great Oak Circle is about 200 feet on your left. The house is on the north side of the road.

Accessibility: A small part of the house can be seen from the street.

■ Maynard Buehler, a University of Iowa Mechanical Engineering graduate, is an inventor of telescopic gun sight mounts. Many of Buehler's ideas have been tested in the machine shop built with the house. In 1948, Buehler sent a photo of the site to Wright. Walter Olds, who was the contractor for the Morris Gift Shop (p28), began construction the same year. Wes Peters from Taliesin, a structural engineer and Wright's son-in-law, assisted with the final planning details. Due to cost the initial floor area was reduced from 4,000 to 2,600 square feet. The original budget was for $25,000 for the house with landscaping, with an overall total of $44,000 for the workshop and furnishings. By 1951, the final figure approached $50,000. The house has been restored since a fire in 1994. c96

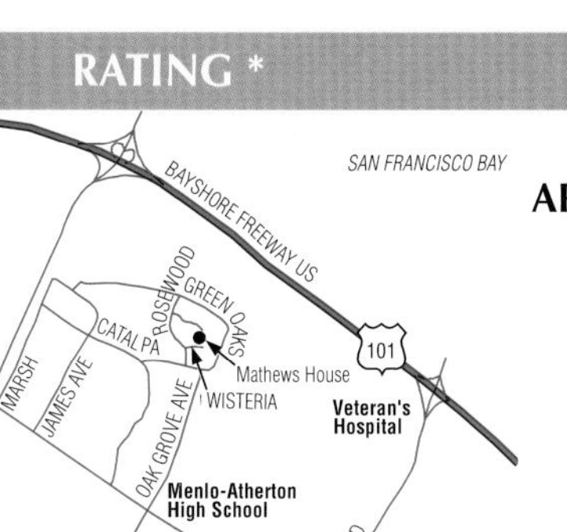

ARTHUR C MATHEWS HOUSE
83 Wisteria Way
Atherton, California 94025
1950 5013

GPS: N 37 28.314
W 122 10.312

Directions: Exit US 101 at Marsh Road and drive to Middlefield Road south to Oak Grove Avenue. Carry on up Oak Grove until reaching a T-junction, where you turn off into Greenoaks Drive and then take right turning into Rosewood Drive. Wisteria Way is the first road on the right.

Accessibility: The house can be seen from the street.

■ The house is red brick as are most of the other Wright designs in the area, such as the Bazett and Hanna Houses (pp32 and 33). The neighborhood has an overgrown, tropical appearance. Very little is known about the Mathews family. c96

In 1955, the Lenkurt Electric Company commissioned Wright to produce a design to the northwest of Atherton at San Mateo (Opus #5520). Founded by Lennart Erickson and Kurt Appert, the company produced microwave telephone equipment. The building was intended for a countryside location on the banks of a lagoon. c96

SIDNEY BAZETT HOUSE
101 Reservoir Road
Hillsborough, California 94010
1939 4002

GPS: N 37 33.268
W 122 20.535

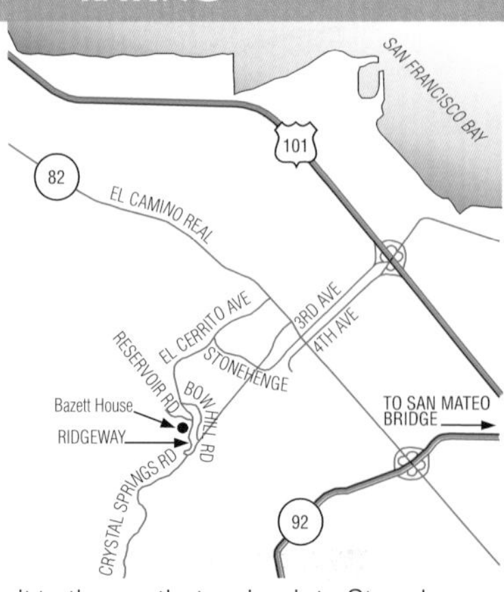

Directions: Exit US 101 at 3rd Avenue and follow it to the north, turning into Stonehenge Road, where it intersects with Crystal Springs Road. Turn left to the west and further up the hill take Ridgeway Road up to Bowhill Road. Where it branches right, turn left onto Reservoir Road and the house will be above you.

Accessibility: The house can be seen from the street.

■ This house is as successful a design as the Hanna House (p33), built on a smaller scale. Sidney Bazett was Vice-President of the Bank of America in San Francisco. The Bazetts, however, divorced and only lived in the house a very short time. In 1945, Louis J Frank, an importer and exporter of dehydrated foods, and his family bought the house and have lived there ever since. The house exists in its original form and condition with the exception of the sleeping porches, which have been enclosed. Wright produced an earlier fir-tree type design for Bazett for a site at Hillsborough (Opus #4032). c94

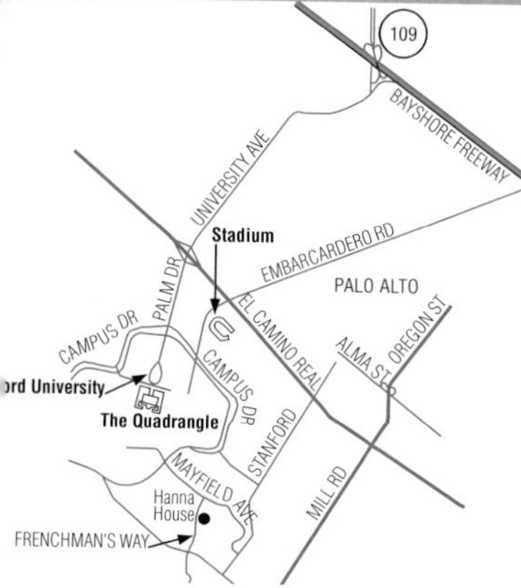

PAUL HANNA (HONEYCOMB) HOUSE
737 Frenchman's Road
Stanford (Palo Alto), California 94305
1937 3701

GPS: N 37 25.168
W 122 09.750

Directions: Exit US 101 at Embarcadero Road and drive west to the Stanford University ring road intersection. Keep south and stay on Campus Drive East as it turns back to the west. Turn off at Mayfield Avenue and continue south toward Gerona Road (Frenchman's Road is one way). Having driven back west on Mayfield watch out for the Frenchman's Road turnoff. The house is on the south side of the street about a block into Frenchman's.

Accessibility: The house can be seen from the street.

■ Jean and Paul Hanna both grew up in Minnesota. Married in 1926, they had three children. When they were both teaching at Columbia, between 1925 and 1935, they came across a review of Wright's Princeton lectures of 1930. They subsequently bought the book of them, *Modern Architecture, Being the Kahn Lectures for 1930*, and sat up all night reading it to each other. They were so taken with it that they wrote to Wright, and met him at Taliesin the following summer on a trip home to Minnesota. Their first plan

was to join up with seven other Columbia colleagues and lease 4 acres from the university. When in 1935, however, Paul joined the Stanford faculty, they stopped at Taliesin for thee days and renewed their interest in building a Wright-designed house, now in California. After producing an extensive and detailed list of the requirements for their new home, Wright designed a two-story house. The drawings for this, however, were returned by the Hannas with an explanation clarifying their position and requesting a single-story house. In January 1936 the Hannas had still not been able to settle on a lot, as Stanford had not confirmed the main water source. Nevertheless, the Hannas invited Wright to come and view the potential building sites at Stanford. During this visit Wright discussed his new geometrical hexagon plan, which the Hannas did not fully comprehend until the drawings arrived. (It was to gain its nickname the Honeycomb House from its adjacent hexagon-shaped grid.) Hanna went to Taliesin to discuss this totally new concept with Wright and the apprentices. The Hannas were very meticulous, they included all their instructions for the house in detailed letters. One Sunday afternoon, when they took their plans to the site to stake out their house on the property, they met a leading geologist who was out walking and inquired what they were doing. When the Hannas told him of their building plans, the geologist explained that a branch of the San Andreas fault ran directly through the hill. When informed of this, Wright responded: 'I built the Imperial Hotel.' After interviewing several contractors, who all declined the job, they found Harold Turner. He went with Hanna to Taliesin to straighten out any misunderstandings. The university, however, still needed to approve the design and Wright personally made the presentation.

In January 1937 the work began. The land lease arrived on the fifteenth. The lease was for twenty years for $100 per year.

During the construction a process developed of hiring new carpenters as the earlier

workforce was reduced through attrition, until a core crew of carpenters was established. The work was explained to the crew and the Hannas through the many trials and tribulations of construction. There were additional costs, and quantities were always larger than anticipated. The Hannas hung on, maintaining their faith throughout. In late November 1937, they moved into the house. When Wright arrived for the weekend on 4 April 1938, with twenty apprentices, he was delighted with the result. He said it was better than he expected it to be.

The house was designed to be altered as the family and their needs changed over time. The children's playroom was to become the formal dining room. Their bedrooms became the home office. Paul added the woodshop and made more furniture according to Wright's drawings. These changes were discussed at great length in an issue of *House Beautiful.* The house is highly adaptable to many different uses. It is a comfortable home for a couple but can also accommodate a reception of a hundred people or more. A wing was added in 1946 (Opus #4607) and the reversion in 1956 (Opus #5634). Each of these changes had to be approved by the university.

Hanna was the Social Studies Editor of the *Worldbook Encyclopedia* for thirty-five years. He led the UNESCO mission to re-establish the educational system in the Philippines after World War II. The Hannas wrote many textbooks and were working on an extensive study on the formation of language at the end of their long lives (Jean died in 1987 and Paul in 1988). Hanna was a member of the famous Hoover Institute. They were both active – still skin-diving in the Caribbean, well into their eighties.

The house is 4,825 square feet. It has ceiling heights varying from from 6 feet 7 inches to 16 feet 3 inches. Though on two levels, it gives the impression of having more stories.

In 1989 the Loma Prieta Earthquake severely damaged the house. The university and other specialists are currently studying how best to repair it. c77

■ Carmel remains a haven for artists of many types. The photographer Ansel Adams lived here for many years, and actor Clint Eastwood thought so much of the community he became mayor. Charles Greene of the famous Pasadena brothers Greene & Greene moved his house and studio here during the 1920s. He built the nearby James House between 1918 and 1923. Several innovative Wright designs were intended for Carmel: the Haldorn House and the small and complex Clark House, as well as the very large Nesbitt House for a beautiful site far up the bay at Cedar Point (see p38 for all these designs). The city is a wonderful place to spend some time. It has great shops with innovative art and a wide beach.

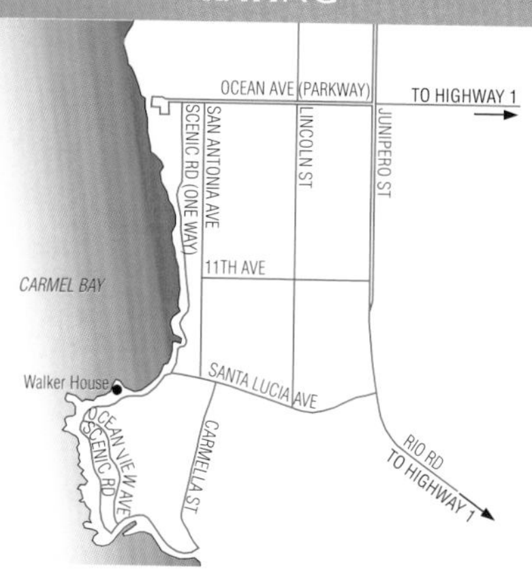

DELLA WALKER HOUSE
Scenic Road at Martin Street
Carmel, California 93921
1951 5122

GPS: N 36 32.703
W 121 55.832

Directions: Exit US 101 at Route 152 to US 1 south. Take the Ocean Avenue turning to Carmel, and drive west to the beach. Follow the Scenic Road to the south to the house.

Accessibility: The house can be seen from the street.

■ On 13 June 1945, Della Walker wrote to Wright requesting a design that would provide protection and privacy. In 1946 she visited Taliesin, producing an endless list of requirements. This list changed frequently, causing disagreements. The new zoning permit of April 1950 allowed the house to be built, the only building on the ocean side of the road in Carmel. From April 1951, the work took nearly two years, costing $125,000. Every query brought construction to a halt: a leaky roof, a smoky fireplace. In 1956 when Della Walker moved in with her new husband, Wright designed an addition. In 1978, on her husband's death the house went to her daughter. Walker's main residence was in Piedmont, California. The interior was a Hollywood set and appears in the 1951 movie *A Summer Place*. c94

CARMEL AND LAKE TAHOE SITES

See map on p36 for locations.

GEORGE CLARK HOUSE SITE, Carmel, California
1951 5112

■ The house is the predecessor to the Boomer House (p76); there is some evidence that the Clark drawings were erased in part and used for the Boomer project. It was titled the 'Sun Bonnet.' It was oriented to the south.

STUART HALDORN HOUSE SITE, Carmel, California
1945 4502

■ Mrs Enid Haldorn was the correspondent for this design. It was published in the January 1948 issue of *Architectural Forum.* The windows were staggered like the Walker House (p37). There was to be a set of stairs tunneling under the road to the rocky shore. The property was later purchased by actress Jean Arthur.

JOHN NESBITT HOUSE SITE, Carmel, California
1940 4017

■ This site was on the point south of the Walker House. The property is located jus south of the 17th green on the Pebble Beach Golf Club. The house was to have a large enclosed garden. John Nesbitt (1911-60), who was a radio personality and movie producer, was prevented from realizing this scheme by the onset of World War II. Nesbitt who won five Oscars in ten years, also owned the Ennis House (p55), in Los Angeles for which he had Wright draw up some improvements (Opus #4006), which also were never built.

LAKE TAHOE SUMMER COLONY SITE, Lake Tahoe, California
1923 2205

■ This scheme was designed for a 200-acre site at Emerald Bay on the southwest c Lake Tahoe. It included a hotel for guests, as well as four types of cabins and three types of barges or floating cabins. The drawings were largely drafted and rendered by Wright himself. A teepee-form design was dated June 1923, and labeled the Wigwam The designs serve as the basis for the Nakoma Country Club (see UGL volume), the Friedman House (p88) and the Richard Davis House (see East volume).

Few documents relating to the scheme survive. The client has not even been identified There is some controversy surrounding the speculative nature of the project and whethe the original client, who may have been Jessie Armstrong (1878-1978), intended to actuall build Wright's designs. Some information suggests that Wright may have attempted t purchase the property for himself. As late as 1933, Wright wrote to Aline Barnsdall an suggested she buy the land. The property was sold in 1928 for $250,000. Wright wa offered the property at $150,000.

ROBERT G WALTON HOUSE
417 Hogue Road
Modesto, California 95350
1957 5623

GPS: N 37 44.938
W 120 59.518

Directions: Take McHenry Avenue north for 4 miles. Turn east on Hogue Road for a quarter mile. The house is on the north side.

Accessibility: The house can not be seen from the street.

■ Born in 1923, in Lancashire, England, Dr Walton attended Guy's Hospital, London. After World War II, he moved to Vancouver, before starting postgraduate work at Stanford, where he heard about the Hanna House. In 1953, he moved to the University of Michigan, where he met his wife. Her brother Douglas Lee had been an apprentice at Taliesin. In 1953, her father commissioned Wright to design a house for him, the Edgar Lee House (Opus #5302). In the same year, Walton decided to locate his new dermatology practice in Modesto, where the couple lived in a hundred-year-old farm house on a property of 42 acres. Despite some skepticism, Walton hired Wright to design them a new house. He was impressed with the professionalism and openness of Wright's methods. c94

RANDALL FAWCETT HOUSE
21200 South Center Avenue
Los Banos, California 93635
1955 5418

GPS: N 37 00.030
W 120 51.133

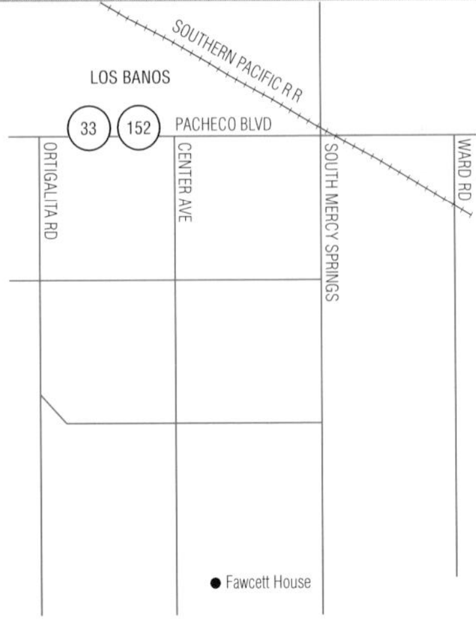

Directions: Take Center Avenue south of Route 152, Pacheco Boulevard for about 5.5 miles. The house is on the east side of the street.

Accessibility: The house can not be seen from the street.

■ The Fawcetts have an extensive dairy farm that surrounds the house. The dairy has a carousel milking machine that turns with the cows on it. The house came about as Randall Fawcett saw the sign identifying the Aaron Green and Frank Lloyd Wright offices in San Francisco (p29, now moved to Pittsburgh) when he was visiting one day and went in out of curiosity. The resident apprentice on this job, Robert Beharka, liked the location so much that he stayed on. He established his own architectural practice in Los Banos, which he continues to this day. c94

NON-URBAN CALIFORNIA SITES

See map on p21 for locations.

JOHNSON DESERT COMPOUND SITE, Death Valley, California 1921 2306

■ Albert M Johnson (1872-1948) was from a wealthy Ohio family, who made their money in mining. He was also the President of the National Life Insurance Company. He took a liking to Walter E Scott (1872-1954), 'Death Valley Scotty,' who staged Wild West dramas, such as the now famous Indian ambush and the phony gold mine. During the 1920s, Johnson's income was between $750,000 and $1 million per annum. After going camping with Scotty in 1906, Johnson started buying land in the area. By 1922, he owned 500 acres. It has been reported that Johnson was involved in borax mining. It is very possible that he was acquainted through his work with John Sukow, the husband of Elizabeth Noble (p51), who was also mining borax in the area at the time.

Johnson met Wright through Alfred MacArthur, a junior officer in the National Life Insurance Company, who owned in Wright's own Oak Park house. MacArthur also knew Gordon Strong of Maryland, who was the client of the Sugarloaf Mountain Project (Opus #2505). Wright received another commission through a partner of Johnson's, LL Nunn, for the Martin Sachse House (Opus #2204).

Johnson, who had already built a simple house and outbuildings on the property, asked Wright for a grander design, which incorporated the existing buildings into a compound including a chapel and main house. Johnson was quite taken by Wright's proposal but remained too timid to build. He eventually paid $3,000,000 for the buildings constructed on this site.

Johnson, who founded the Gospel Foundation, gave the Death Valley land to them after his death in 1948. The foundation sold it to the National Park Service in 1970, and it is now open to the public.

FRANK LLOYD WRIGHT DESERT COMPOUND SITE, Mojave, California 1924 2107

■ The exact site for this project is unknown, but may have been at or near the Johnson work. Wright noted on a drawing that he had identified a residence for himself in the desert. It had something he termed a 'cool patio.' This device was also used as the major space at the Harold Price House in Phoenix (p81). The drawings are sketchy and the attribution is uncertain. It may have been intended for a location other than the Death Valley desert.

YOSEMITE NATIONAL PARK RESTAURANT SITE, Yosemite, California 1954 5307

■ This circular building was executed for Degnan Donahoe Inc, a franchise food provider to the Park. It was, however, said to have competed with the natural beauty of the park to such an extent that it caused political powers to intervene and force the design to be abandoned. *Food Service* magazine featured this design in its November 1958 issue.

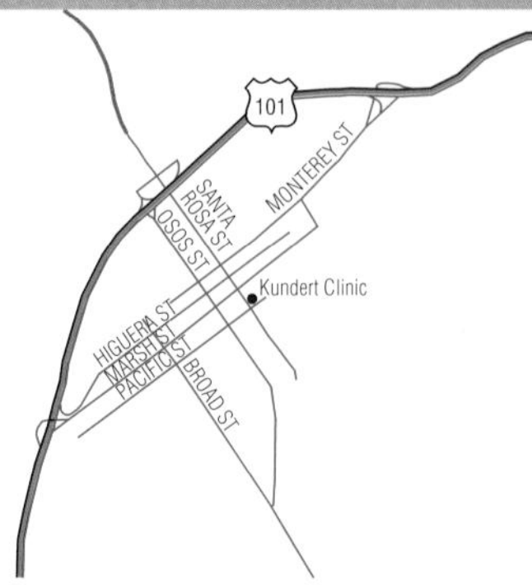

KUNDERT MEDICAL CLINIC
1106 Pacific Street
San Luis Obispo, California 93401
1956 5614

GPS: N 35 16.849
W 120 39.416

Directions: Exit US 101 at Osos Street and drive south for 0.5 miles or seven blocks to Pacific Steet and turn east two blocks to Santa Rosa Steet. The clinic is on the corner.

Accessibility: The clinic can be seen from the Street.

■ In 1950, an extensive study was begun to determine how Dr Kundert's patients should be received. Plans for the building, however, were not started until 1954. The receptionist's desk was to be positioned in the center of the clinic to direct the office traffic. The original building design was to be constructed of custom-made concrete blocks, but the local building code would not permit them so brick was used. Aaron Green supervised the work during the five-month construction period. The plan is unusual in the way that it eradicated hallways by placing all the practice rooms off a central waiting room. The focus of the main space is out toward the creek where there is an outside patio. The office was also originally used by a dentist and an optometrist. c77

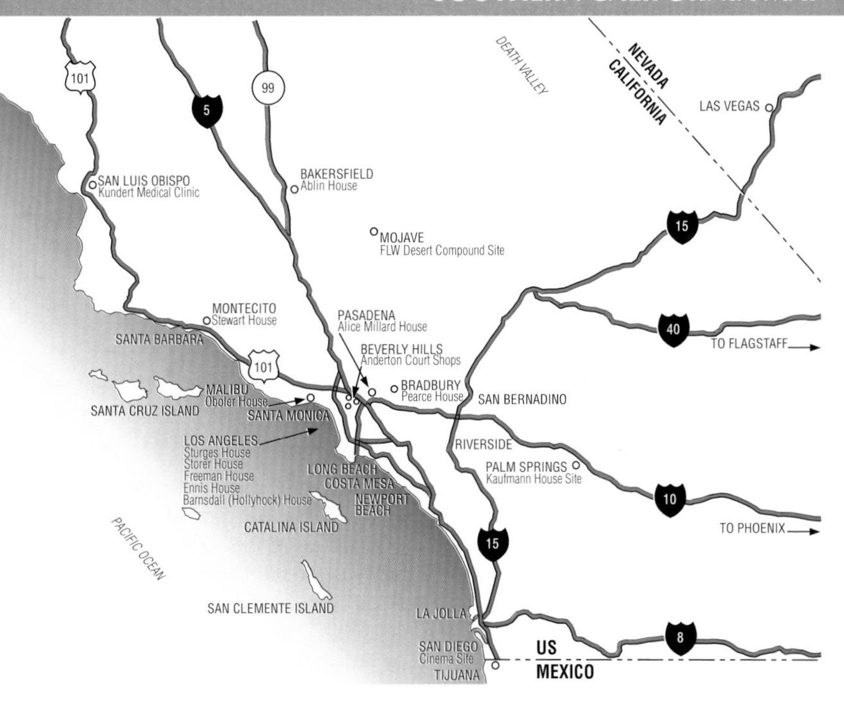

■ Wright was preceded to Southern California by his sons, who worked in architectural practices out here. Lloyd worked on many of Wright's Los Angeles designs, as well as those prepared in Los Angeles for Chandler, near Phoenix (p83). The majority of Wright's buildings form a band that can be traced across from Bradbury on the east, through Pasadena and Beverly Hills to Montecito on the west, and across the north of Los Angeles.

SOUTHERN CALIFORNIA SITES

EDGAR J KAUFMANN HOUSE SITE, Palm Springs, California 1951 5111

■ Liliane rather than Edgar Kaufmann Jr was probably the main client. The house was intended for a site near Neutra's design of 1946. Though the general contractor, CG Chamberlin, was ready to begin building on 14 February 1951, having purchased some materials, it remained unbuilt. Liliane Kaufmann died on 7 September 1951.

CINEMA SITE, San Diego, California 1905 0517

■ The client and site are unknown. Early for a movie theater, it was conceived long before either of Wright's architect sons was working in the area. The facade has similar tiles to those used in the Coonley House of 1908 (see MetroChicago volume).

GEORGE C STEWART HOUSE
196 Hot Springs Road
Montecito, California 93103
1909 0907

GPS: N 34 25.516
W 119 38.849

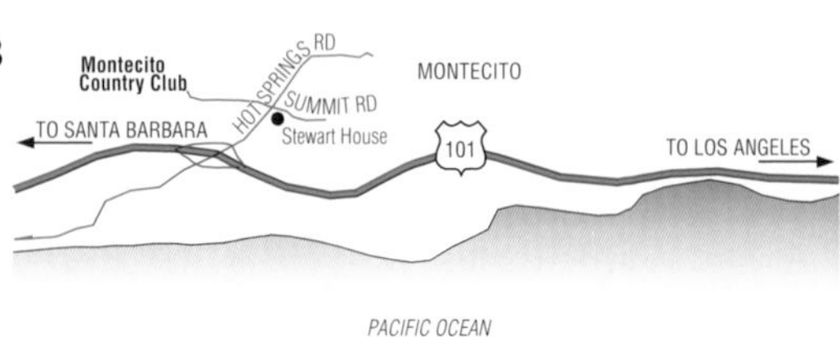

Directions: Exit US Route 101 at Hot Springs Road and drive north for 0.4 miles. The house is just before the turning for Summit Road.

Accessibility: The house can be seen from the street.

■ George Stewart (1879-1965) was an accountant from Edinburgh, Scotland, whose wife Emily (1879-1920) had an interest in the arts. Emily was probably responsible for engaging Wright. Her family had owned the house's site since 1894 and gave it to them as a wedding gift. Her family, the Oothout family, started the Thompson Seedless Grape in the Fresno area with the Galbraiths. First noted at this address in the 1917-18 city directory, George Stewart was last listed at it in 1939. Unfortunately there is no surviving correspondence between the Stewarts and Wright, and there is no indication that Wright ever visited the building. This is the earliest Wright building in California and only his second west of the Mississippi River. The Stewarts had other houses in Fresno, Los Angeles and San Francisco. This was not their primary residence. c75

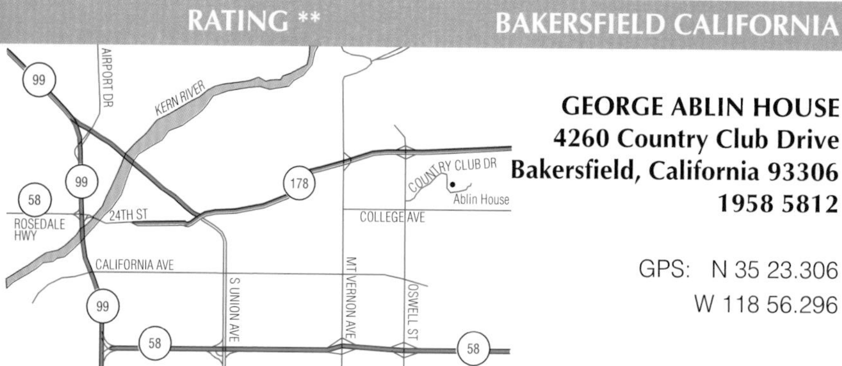

GEORGE ABLIN HOUSE
4260 Country Club Drive
Bakersfield, California 93306
1958 5812

GPS: N 35 23.306
W 118 56.296

Directions: Exit Highway 99 (parallel to Interstate 5 and just north of the southern intersection of 5 and 99) at Route 178, Crosstown City Freeway. Drive eastbound on Route 178 for 3.5 miles to Oswell Street, then turn off south for 0.8 miles to Country Club Drive. Once on the drive follow its curves along to number 4260. The house is on the east side of the street at the Claremont Drive intersection.

Accessibility: Over a small rise behind landscaping, the house cannot be seen from the street.

■ George Ablin is a neuro surgeon from Chicago. In the fifties, when he was searching for a city to set up his practice, he chose Bakersfield primarily for its climate and industry. The Ablins originally wrote to Wright on a lark. Built to accommodate the Ablin's seven children, the house is 2,000-square feet. The purple flecks in the custom-made concrete blocks match the color of the facing mountains. At the time of its construction, there was only one other dwelling in the neighborhood. A local junior college built the metal entry gate to Wright's design. The dining-room furniture is original. c96

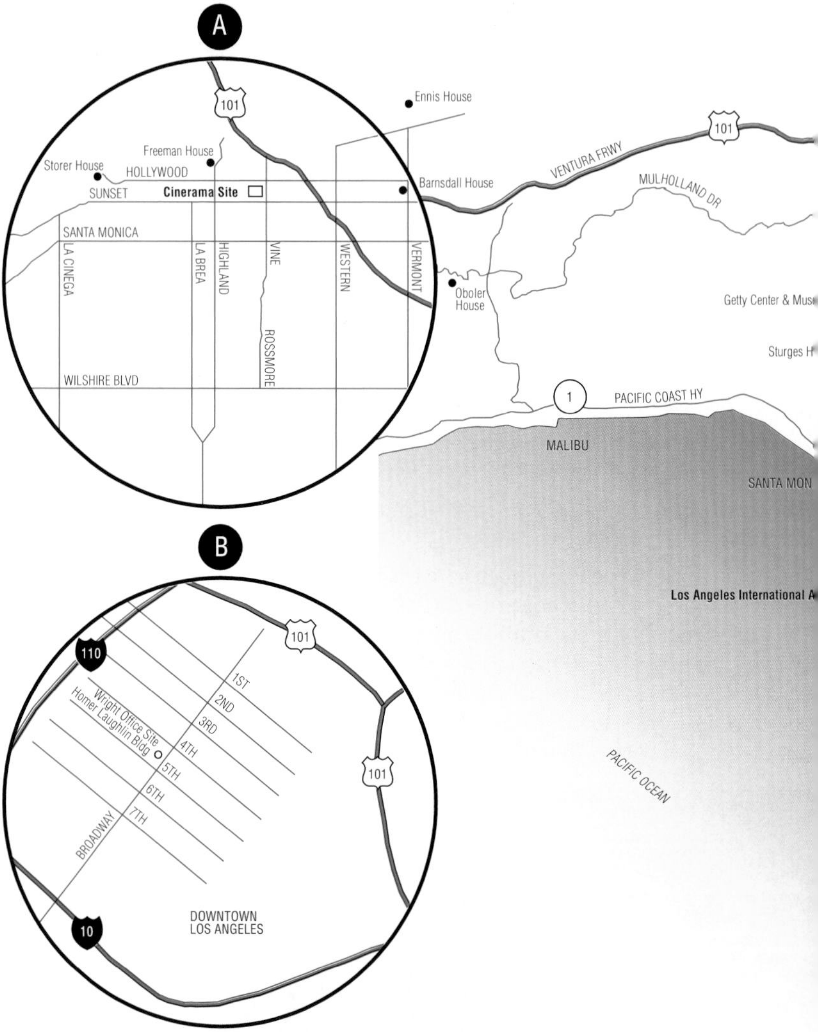

■ Los Angeles has always been an exciting town to be a part of, even as a visitor. It has maintained its charm, glamor and mystery, mixing many cultures from across the border and across the ocean. Like the older cities of the east, most of the buildings in Los Angeles can be seen from the street. The drive from the Anderton Court Shops (p50) in Beverly Hills east to the Hollyhock House and onto Pasadena is a beautiful one. It gives some of the best views of the Los Angeles basin, as one can see all the way to Catalina Island on a clear day.

Two of Wright's largest schemes in Los Angeles, the Doheny Ranch Project and the Huntington Hartford Resort (p51) would have been built on adjacent sites. Their realization may have inextricably changed the direction of the city's architecture, altering the planning and the character of large projects. Unfortunately, there is no space here to note the associated buildings of Wright's sons and assistants, such as the Austrian emigrés Rudolph Schindler (1887-1953) and Richard Neutra (1892-1970). Lloyd's own studio on Doheny Drive, built out of special concrete block, is also worthy of inclusion.

ARCH OBOLER GATEHOUSE
32436 West Mulholland Highway
Malibu, California 90265
1941 4112, 4602, 5508

GPS: N 34 06.012
W 118 50.607

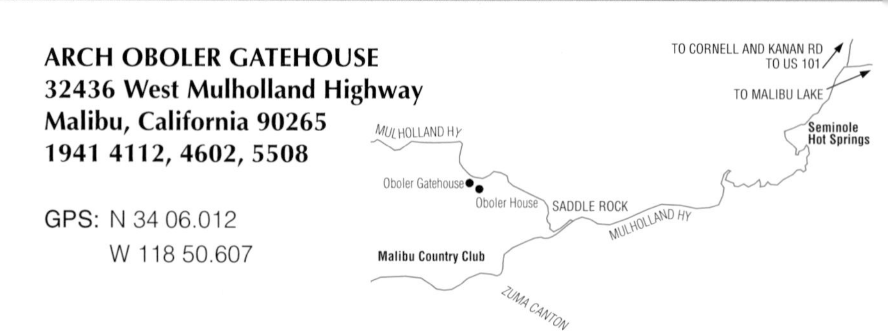

Directions: Exit US Route 101 at Kanan Road, N9, south for 6.1 miles to Mulholland Highway and turn west for 2.2 miles to the house. It is on the south side of the street.

Accessibility: The gatehouse and other built structures can be seen from the street.

■ Arch Oboler was studying Electrical Engineering at the University of Chicago when he first encountered the Robie House. This started him out on a life-long interest in Wright. In 1934, the sale of a story called 'Futuristic' to NBC launched him on a career writing radio dramas. Oboler's other successes included 'Lights Out' and 'Inner Sanctum.' Before moving to Malibu, he lived in a New York brownstone with a pet rabbit. Though the gatehouse, retreat and studio were built, the main house, 'Eaglefeather' (Opus #4018), was never realized. Oboler lived here until his death in 1987. c96

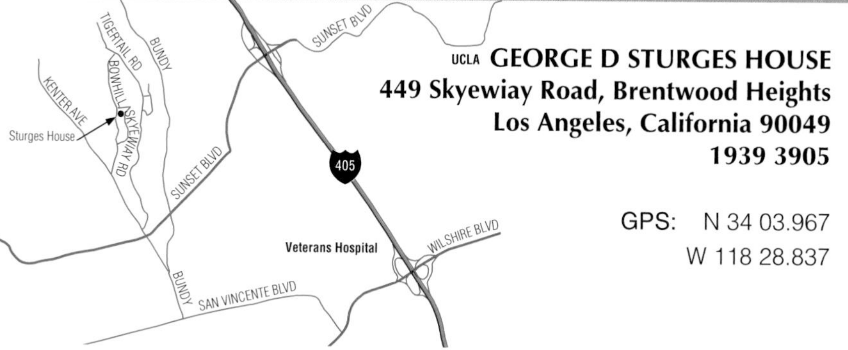

UCLA **GEORGE D STURGES HOUSE**
449 Skyewiay Road, Brentwood Heights
Los Angeles, California 90049
1939 3905

GPS: N 34 03.967
W 118 28.837

Directions: Exit Interstate 405 at Sunset Boulevard west and drive for 1.2 miles to Kenter Avenue. Keep going north on Kenter for 0.4 miles to Skyewiay Road.

Accessibility: The house can be seen from the street.

■ This house was meant to be the design model for the young American couple. It was developed from the first design for Malcom Willey of Minneapolis (see UGL volume). As a result of the innovative wood roof and canted walls, however, the house leaked so severely on its completion that Sturges, an engineer for the Lockheed Company, installed a series of rain funnels. Later John Lautner, the successful Los Angeles architect and one of Wright's early apprentices, and the current owner developed the metal flashing system and reinforced the trellis with steel supports. The living room was so low that Sturges, who was tall, had to duck to traverse it. When the Sturgeses found the two-bedroom house too small for their growing family, a woman architect designed another house for them on 741 Tiger Tail, one valley to the west. She included in it a copy of the Wright-designed living room but with a heightened ceiling. c80

ANDERTON COURT SHOPS
332 North Rodeo Drive
Beverly Hills, California 90210
1952 5032

GPS: N 34 04.148
W 118 24.017

Directions: Exit Interstate 405 at Santa Monica Boulevard and go east for 3 miles to Rodeo Drive south. Once on Rodeo, drive for a quarter of a mile to the shops on the west side of the street.

Accessibility: The shops can be seen from the street.

■ Born in Wisconsin, Nina Goldbine Anderton (1889-1979) was married to Raymond Anderton (1898-1979), who owned the Maanexit Spinning Company of Providence, Rhode Island. Though she disagreed with Wright on most occasions, concerning the design and construction of this small shopping precinct, both persevered and completed the project. The building appears a bit gaudier than it did originally due to the size, position and color of the present signs. After Raymond's death, Nina married Richard Winans who also preceded her. She lived in Bel-Air but was robbed several times, once while giving a dinner party. Later, she moved to a Westwood high-rise. She worked for several charities, including the City of Hope. Anderton, who kept her first married name, is buried in the Anderton family plot of the Swan Point Cemetery in Providence. c95

LOS ANGELES AREA SITES

See map on pp46-47 for locations.

DOHENY RANCH PROJECT SITE, Beverly Hills, California 1923 2104

■ The project was designed for Edward Laurence Doheny (1856-1935), who struck oil in Los Angeles in 1892 with Charles Caufield. Both men's incomes exceeded $500,000 and approached $1 million per year after 1900. Doheny was involved in the Teapot Dome scandal of 1922-24, although he was not convicted of any wrongdoing. He bought the 411-acre site, just east of Beverly Crest, in 1912. The site extended north and slightly west of the intersection of Hillcrest Drive and Sunset Boulevard at Coldwater Canyon. It was a long and narrow piece of land that was completely assembled by February 1923. Doheny was a friend of Albert Einstein and was responsible for bringing him west in 1933.

HUNTINGTON HARTFORD RESORT SITE, Beverly Hills, California 1947 4721 and 4737

■ George Huntington Hartford II, the heir to the Atlantic & Pacific Tea Company, was born in 1911. An ensign in the Coast Guard during World War II, he involved himself in artistic ventures after leaving the services. He started a modeling agency in 1947 and began producing movies and theater. In 1954, he opened his own Broadway theater with a show starring Helen Hayes (Charles McArthur's wife, see p74). The resort was to include tournament tennis, a swimming pool and a cinema. Zoning restrictions, however, prevented it from being built. Hartford's own residence was to be a part of the three-lobed cantilevered construction at the highest part of the proposed complex.

ELIZABETH NOBLE APARTMENTS SITE, Alcot Steet at 1426 Edris Avenue (near Beverly Drive and Pico Boulevard), Los Angeles, California 1929 2903

■ Harold F McCormick (1872-1941) paid for the design of the apartments but eventually built a different house on the same site by another architect for Elizabeth Noble. This house has now been demolished. McCormick had been a client for a site in Lake Forest, Illinois (Opus #0713), two years after he became treasurer of his father's International Harvester Corporation in Chicago. McCormick, who met Noble in Los Angeles, was quite enamored with her. She, however, decided that she did not want to be a landlord and did not want to manage an apartment building. Noble's ex-husband, a physician named John Sukow, had been involved in borax mining in Mojave in 1913 and later in Bakersfield. Her daughter became a physician.

FRANK LLOYD WRIGHT OFFICE SITE, 522 Homer Laughlin Building, 315 South Broadway, Los Angeles 90013

■ Wright occupied this space, where his son Lloyd and Rudolph Schindler were located, for only several months while the Barnsdall project was under construction (pp56-60), previous to his move to the Harper Studio. Schindler is known to have written to Louis Sullivan in Chicago from here. Harrison Albright (1866-1933), Wright's contact for the San Francisco Call Building project (p29), had offices in this building from 1905 until his retirement in 1925.

FRANK LLOYD WRIGHT STUDIO SITE,1284 Harper, Los Angeles 1922 2201 studio graphics

■ Only built in 1922, Wright's offices occupied the building in March 1923. The Harper Studio was intended to be temporary until a more permanent studio was constructed in Beverly Hills. Schindler's own Kings Road House is six blocks to the southwest.

TODD A-O THEATERS SITES 1958 5819 and 5829

■ Michael Todd was the main force behind this project. He wanted to create a design for a chain of movie theaters with domes by Richard Buckminster Fuller (1895-1983), fabricated out of aluminum tubing and skin provided by Henry J Kaiser (1882-1967) of Oakland, California, of automobile and aluminum fame. Another team member was Pat Weaver of NBC, who was to provide expertise on the viability of the entertainment value. Wright was brought in to pull together the design and its overall effect. One theater with a geodesic design, the Cinerama, was built in 1963 in Hollywood. Situated on Sunset Boulevard near Vine Street, it had 937 seats and 316 concrete panels. Todd was also in the process of developing a wide picture format with American Optical. (The picture *Oklahoma* was the first to adopt this format, which is now widely used.) Born Avrom Hirsch Goldbogen, in either December 1908 or June 1909, he changed his name to Michael Todd. His father was a Polish rabbi who emigrated to Minneapolis and moved to Chicago in 1918. Todd was killed in a plane crash on 22 March 1958, near Grants, New Mexico, on his way to New York to a dinner at the Waldorf-Astoria. At the time of his death, Todd was married to actress Elizabeth Taylor, who had accompanied him on visits to Taliesin West during the design process.

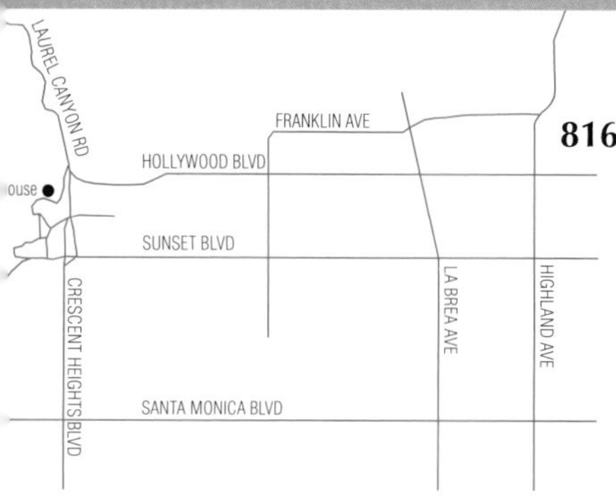

JOHN STORER HOUSE
8161 Hollywood Boulevard, Hollywood
Los Angeles, California 90069
1923 2304

GPS: N 34 06.052
W 118 22.035

Directions: Take Laurel Canyon Road north at its intersection with Hollywood Boulevard. To access the westbound Hollywood Boulevard extension, do a U-turn southbound. It exits southbound Laurel Canyon at a traffic light 100 feet south of the U-turn and is not well marked. Go up the hill and around the corner a few hundred feet to the house.

Accessibility: The house can be seen from the street.

■ The house may have been built on speculation by the Superior Building Company. Dr John Storer (1868-1933), who lived in the house until 1927, was a real estate developer involved with the company. Building work began at the beginning of November 1923. Lloyd Wright took over from the original contractor, AC Pardee, in December 1923. The design was originally proposed for Charles Lowes of Eagle Rock (Opus #2202). The four bedrooms are on two floors on the west side of the house, the living room is at the center next to the bedrooms and above the dining room. The kitchen is on the east side. The house has recently been restored by movie producer Joel Silver. In 1944, *Fountainhead* author Ayn Rand nearly bought the house. c85

SAMUEL FREEMAN HOUSE
1962 Glencoe Way
Los Angeles, California 90028
1924 2402

GPS: N 34 06.370
W 118 20.305

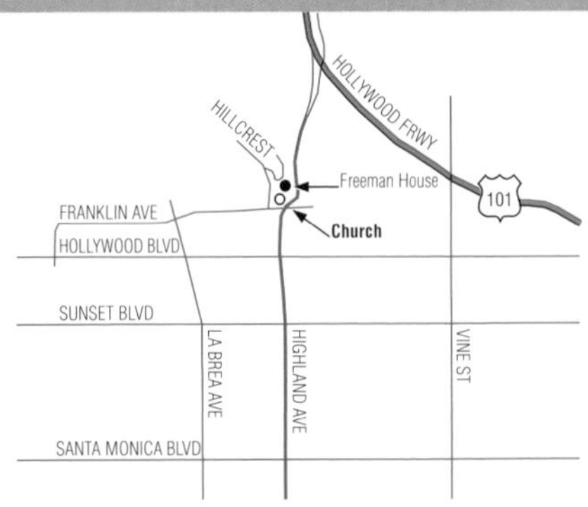

Directions: Drive north of Hollywood and Sunset Boulevards, which run parallel at the north end of Highland Avenue, turning off west to Franklin Avenue. Go only one short block to Hillcrest Road and up a steep hill to Glencoe Way. Turn east.

Accessibility: The house can be seen from the street.

■ The Freemans lived in their house from its construction until their deaths. Married in 1921, Sam (1889-1981) was a jeweler and Harriett (1890-1986) was a modern dancer, both were active in social causes. Harriett was a relative of the Lovells of the Neutra Lovell Health House (1927). The lot is one of the smallest at about 70 by 80 feet, but the view to the south on Highland Avenue is spectacular. With the drawings completed in early 1924, the building permit was issued on 8 April. The house was finished on 23 March 1925 after several liens were satisfied, work having been stopped a few times due to lack of funds. This is the first of Wright's houses to have mitered corner glass windows. Harriett became involved with Rudolph Schindler, who was working for Wright; he designed much of the furniture and did some minor remodeling in the bedroom. c78

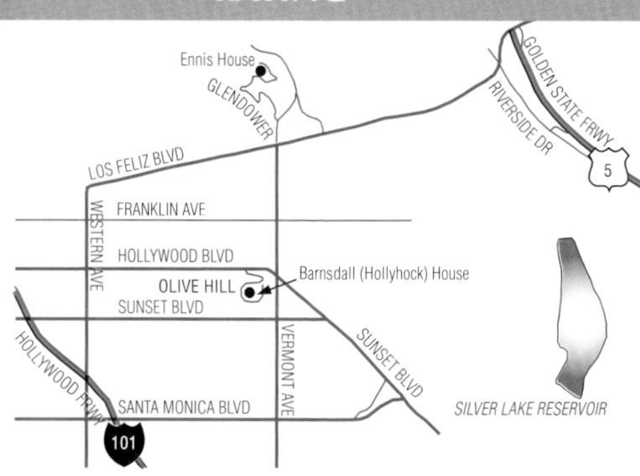

CHARLES ENNIS HOUSE
2655 Glendower Avenue
Los Angeles, California 90027
1923 2401

GPS: N 34 06.985
W 118 17.554

Directions: Go north on Vermont Avenue from Hollywood Boulevard and cross Los Feliz Boulevard one block to the crossover. Keep right and enter onto Glendower Avenue. Take Glendower as it turns back and forth up the hill to the house.

Accessibility: The house can be seen from the street. Tours are available.

■ Charles Ennis (1858-1928) moved with his wife to Los Angeles in 1901. Ennis had a clothing store. The house is 248 feet long on a half acre site at the top of a ridge east of Mount Hollywood Observatory. The construction began in March 1924 with Lloyd Wright as the contractor and landscape designer. The Ennises took over the work when Lloyd resigned after several disputes. The house was completed in September 1926.

In 1940, the house was purchased by John Nesbitt (1910-60), a movie producer at MGM, who asked for Wright's help furnishing the interior. In 1941, Wright sent drawings for new ceilings and a full set of furniture. With assistance from Lloyd, a swimming pool was installed along the north wall. The house been the setting for many movies, including *Blade Runner* and *Supergirl*. The Barnsdall House is directly to the south of it. c79

ALINE BARNSDALL (HOLLYHOCK) HOUSE
4808 Hollywood Boulevard
Los Angeles, California 90027
1917 1705

GPS: N 34 06.015
W 118 17.658

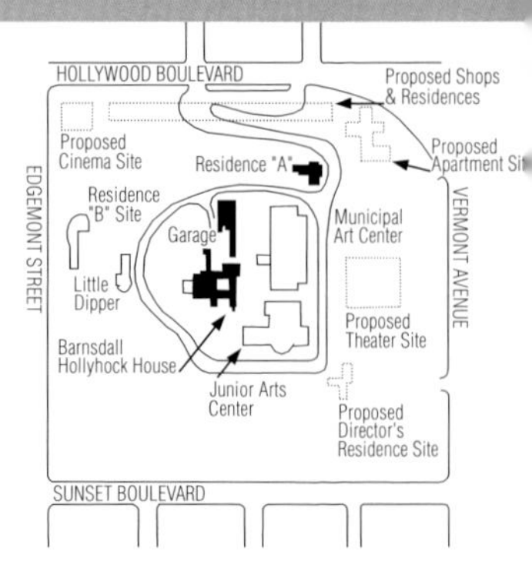

Directions: Take Hollywood Boulevard one block west of Vermont Avenue to the entry to Barnsdall Park. Go up the hill and around to the house and other buildings.

Accessibility: The house can be seen through the fence. Tours of the interior are available.

■ Louisa Aline Barnsdall (1882-1946) was the heiress to a fortune accumulated by a wealthy oil family from Titusville, Pennsylvania. On the death of her father in 1917, she was left over $6 million. Emotionally volatile and often difficult, Barnsdall was also a passionate social and political activist. First caught up in the theater in New York, she moved to Chicago in search of a less snobbish place to produce and direct an experimental theater company. In about 1914, she met Wright there – she had in fact initially contacted Wright after his return from Europe in 1911, though their first meeting did not occur until she bumped into him in Mrs Potter Palmer's garage at this time. By 1915, Barnsdall had engaged his services to design a theater in Chicago. After traveling to the West Coast, however, she became enamored with Los Angeles and bought 35

acres of an olive orchard on a hill in an otherwise flat part of town and moved to the city. She persisted in her request for a theater design from Wright but was dissatisfied with the initial drawings. In the summer of 1916, her Los Angeles company had its first season in a rented auditorium there. The young playwright and set designer Norman Bel Geddes was hired to assist in the scenery and Richard Ordynski, the theater director, helped her direct. She had an affair with Ordynski, and in August 1917 gave birth to his child, Louise Aline George, 'Betty' or 'Sugar Top.'

Barnsdall commissioned from Wright a grand home for herself and her daughter in Los Angeles. The Hollyhock House was built between 1919 and 1921 on a 36-acre site on Olive Hill. Wright designed not only the main residence but also several other buildings, including a theater, townhouses, a director's residence 'A,' and artists' residence 'B,' a kindergarten, shops and a cinema.

Lloyd Wright was the on-site superintendent until he literally threw the contractor in to the pool and was replaced by Rudolph Schindler. The house was constructed of hollow

clay tiles with stucco surfacing. The ornament is concrete, or cast stone as it was then known. The foundations were concrete and brick. At the time of the construction of the house, Los Angeles was still considered a desert locale with a harsh climate – sunshine was yet to be regarded as healthy. The windows are small and deep set, compared with the slightly later buildings that incorporated full walls of glass.

The arrangement of the courtyard and the use of the roofs were designed to accommodate theatrical programs. The pools on the east and west were once connected to the pool around the living-room fireplace as part of a stream with lakes that flowed through the entire property. The mural over the fireplace was described by Lloyd, as Barnsdall as an Indian princess on a throne surveying her lands. Unlike the many Prairie Houses, which Wright had built over a decade previously in and around Chicago, where the fireplace is at the center of the plan, the fireplace here is off axis. The colors of the house's interior were specified as mauve with blue, golden brown and mulberry (nearly Chinese red). Hollyhocks were said to have been Aline's favorite flower. They were used as both the decorative theme as well as the title of the house. (Wright first referred to it as the Hollyhock House in his 1932 *Autobiography*, in all the official documents for the job it is referred to as the 'Owner's Residence'.) There are abstractions of the hollyhock in art glass and concrete on both the exterior and interior. They form a decorative band around the outside window heads. The arrangement and furnishings of the rooms make the house appear to be smaller than its actual dimensions. The dining table sits six people and the living room arrangement also sits six comfortably.

Although there were many disagreements between Wright and Barnsdall, they must have made up as her daughter Betty attended the school at Taliesin during the 1930s.

In December 1923 Barnsdall announced her donation of 10 acres of Olive Hill and the Hollyhock House to the City of Los Angeles. In 1927 the city took on the property as a public art park. Barnsdall continued to use the house on her occasional visits to Los Angeles. When the Barnsdall Oil Refinery, just north of the city, was shelled by the Japanese in February 1942, it made headlines. The house fell into disrepair. After the war, Mrs Dorothy Clune Murray leased the house from the city for use as an arts center in memory of her son, who died in Eastern France in 1944 at the age of twenty-one. Edmund Teske, who was the official Taliesin photographer, moved into Studio Residence B in 1943 and continued to live there until 1949. It was he who found Aline dead in the house on 18 December 1946. She was sixty-three years old.

The buildings were restored by Lloyd Wright and his architect son, Eric, in the early 1970s. c77-85

OLIVE HILL

See site plan on p56 for locations.

STUDIO RESIDENCE A, 1645 North Vermont Avenue, Los Angeles 1920 2002

■ The building permit for the residence was issued on 29 December 1920, with the construction costs estimated at $18,000. The Walter C and Louise Arensburg family, who had a famous contemporary art collection including works by Marcel Duchamp and other modern artists now in the Philadelphia Art Museum, lived here a short time in about 1921 or 1922. Ever since it became part of Barnsdall's gift to the city, the building has been used as an arts and crafts center.

STUDIO RESIDENCE B SITE, Barnsdall Park, Los Angeles 1920 2003

■ This design was quite unlike Wright's other works. It used lapped boards as borders and had a courtyard, similar in many ways to the later work of Rudolph Schindler. Three bedrooms were laid out over two floors and there was a double-story living room. The dining-room furniture is now in the Hollyhock House. The entry columns were decorated with stencils and a color line that included rose, bronze, gray-blue and pale yellows. Wright moved from the Harper Avenue Studio and rented this house as his residence and office from August to December 1923, after which he moved to the Beverly Hills Hotel. In 1928, Aline Barnsdall took up residence here after she gave the main house to the City of Los Angeles. Schindler remodeled the studio at this time. In the late 1920s, Residence B was also used as a UCLA fraternity house. Edmund Teske lived here from 1944 to 1949 (see p58). The demolition permit was issued on 11 March 1954. c77-85

LITTLE DIPPER SITE, Barnsdall Park, Los Angeles
1921 2301

■ The kindergarten was begun after the building permit #53 782 was issued on 7 November 1923. It was to be built at an estimated cost of $12,500. Construction was, however, stopped by the City of Los Angeles on 22 November 1922. The building department wanted some changes that Barnsdall did not want to pay for. Work had progressed as far as the foundations, 226 blocks had also been laid out of the 7,508 manufactured. It was intended to be a progressive school for twenty students, including Barnsdall's daughter. The contractor was AC Parlee, who also worked on the Millard House at this time. Portions of the original work remains on the west side of the drive west of the Hollyhock House.

SCHEMES FOR OLIVE HILL SITE, Barnsdall Park, Los Angeles
1920 2005

■ Opus #2005 covers all the designs for Barnsdall that have not been allocated separate opus numbers by the Frank Lloyd Wright Foundation. The larger scheme for the development of Olive Hill was to include a 'legitimate' theater aligned with the Hollyhock House on the eastern slope. Shops and housing, in terraced dwellings and an apartment building at the northeast corner, were to be provided for those working in the theater. Another residence for the director was intended for a site southeast of Hollyhock House.

A small building that comes under this opus number, which was realized, is the Spring House. It was intended to regulate the flow of water within the site. It remains 'hidden' inside the crafts center behind a gate.

MOTION PICTURE THEATER SITE, Barnsdall Park, Los Angeles
1920 2007

■ This was to be located at the northwest corner of the site, north of the site of Residence B. In the 1950s, Kenneth Ross, the Director of Parks, asked Wright for a design of the new art gallery (Opus #5428) for the eastern side of Olive Hill. This request came after a large show of Wright's work, 'Sixty Years of Living Architecture', was exhibited in a special pavilion adjacent to Hollyhock House (Opus #5427). Ross saw a need for a large permanent facility, but the budget was too small and the needs too large at that time. Another building was built on the same site in 1971, which is now known as the Barnsdall Park Gallery, the Municipal Art Gallery. Its neighbor, the Junior Arts Center, was erected in 1967. They are open on a regular basis as an art museum and educational facility.

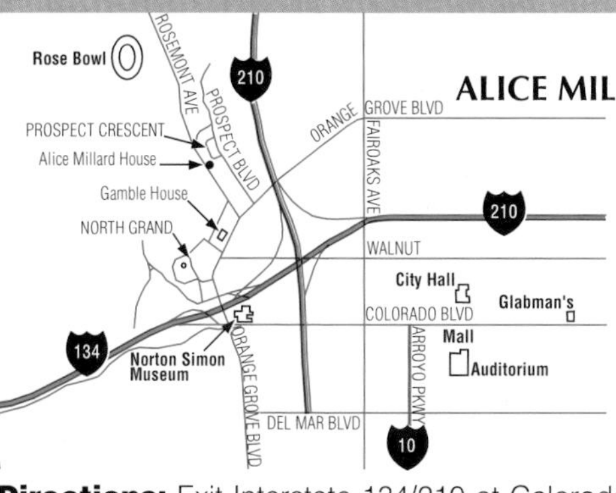

ALICE MILLARD (LA MINIATURA) HOUSE

645 Prospect Circle
Pasadena, California 91103
1923 2302

GPS: N 34 09.372
W 118 09.686

Directions: Exit Interstate 134/210 at Colorado Boulevard and drive north two long blocks along Orange Grove Boulevard North to Rosemont Avenue. Once on Rosemont keep west for about two blocks.

Accessibility: The house is visible from the street on both sides.

■ Alice Parsons Millard (1873-1938) was married to George Madison Millard (1846-1918), who had already had a Wright house built for them in Highland Park, Illinois (see MetroChicago volume), in 1906. In 1908 they moved to Las Flores in South Pasadena. After the death of George, Alice kept on with their rare book business, expanding it to include European antiques. Millard was persuaded to buy a lot in a small ravine. Wright took on the construction of the house for a guaranteed price, though it ran over budget. The building started in March of 1923 with AC Parlee as contractor for $9,810. Millard bought another lot to the east, and one directly to the north that remains vacant. Lloyd Wright designed a gallery addition (Opus #2503) in 1926. Wright designed a speculative house for the rose garden site to the west of Lloyd's addition (Opus #3421). c79

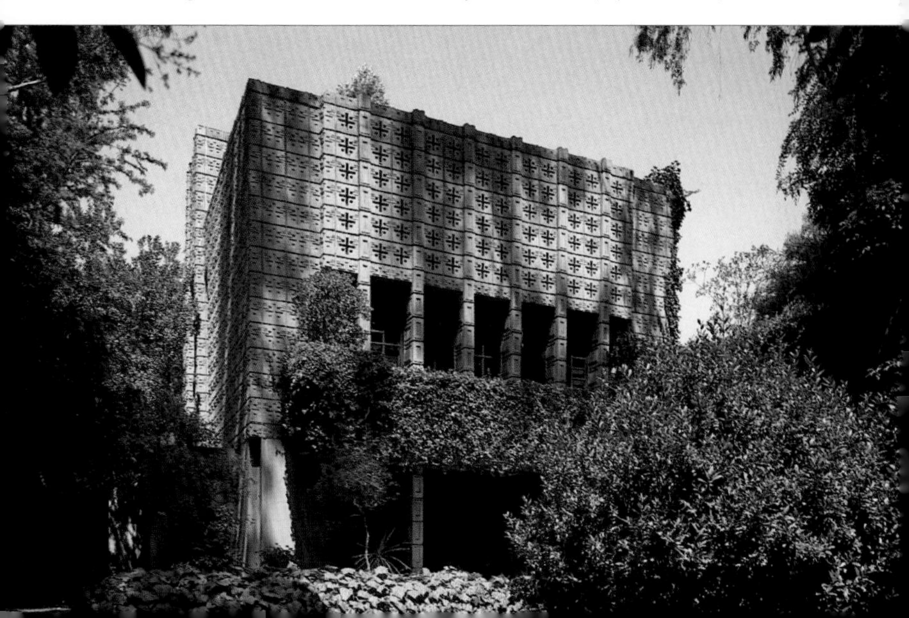

WILBUR PEARCE HOUSE
5 Bradbury Hills Road
Bradbury, California 91010
1951 5114

GPS: N 34 08.808
W 117 57.883

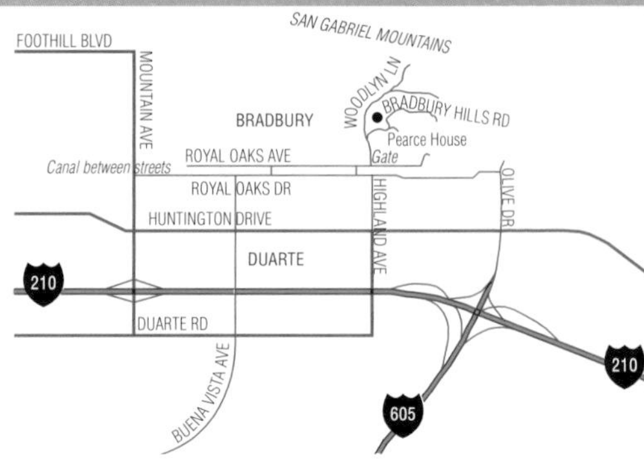

Directions: Exit Interstate 210 at Buena Vista Avenue, drive northbound half a mile t Royal Oaks Drive. Turn east for 1.1 miles to Highland Avenue. When at the top of Highlanc turn left onto Oak Avenue and then right onto Oaks Drive. Take the first left, Woodly Lane. Bradbury Hills Road is off Woodlyn to the right.

Accessibility: The house is in a private gated neighborhood.

■ In 1950, Wilbur Pearce's ill health brought the Pearces to the Los Angeles area fror Akron, Ohio, where Pearce was Assistant Sales Manager to the Firestone Rubbe Company. Pearce and Wright had been friends since 1930. When President of th Women's Art League of Akron, in 1945, Elizabeth Pearce invited Wright to talk to he group. In 1951, the Pearces commissioned Wright to design this $15,000 house. Wrigh designed the fascia to be tilted (angled), and Pearce agreed; six clients had alread previously declined this feature. The Pearces were early residences of Bradbury an campaigned to preserve the town by relocating a proposed freeway further south. Th house is 102 feet long with an 80-foot curved wall. The windows are 13 feet high. c8

■ The states of the western mountains and plains included here – Montana, Wyoming, Idaho, Utah, Arizona, Colorado, New Mexico, Nebraska, Kansas, Oklahoma and Texas – form a disparate group. They contain both the tallest building Wright designed, the Price Tower (p92), and the smallest dwellings, the Como Orchards Cottages (p66), which are probably also the least visited. Many of these buildings are difficult to locate even with a map. The roads change frequently as improvements are made, going unrecorded on major state maps. The author's ratings for these are low, not because they are bad designs, but because of the effort it takes to get to them. The majority of clients in this area were not wealthy. They tended to have the notion of hiring an architect who would be able to both realize their ideas in physical form and satisfy their domestic requirements.

LOCKRIDGE MEDICAL CLINIC
341 Central Avenue
Whitefish, Montana 59937
1958 5813

GPS: N 48 24.541
W 114 20.191

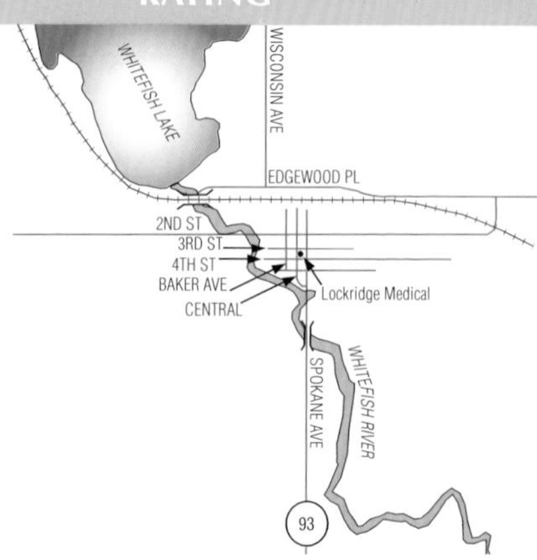

Directions: Whitefish is in northern Montana near the western border, north of Missoula. The building is easy to locate, two blocks west of Highway 93, 2nd Street and one block west of Spokane Avenue on Central Avenue. It is in the center of the block on the east side of the street.

Accessibility: The building can be seen from the street.

■ Dr T Leon Lockridge was a friend of Wright's. Born in 1912, in Rawlins, Montana, he grew up in Whitefish. Having attended high school there, he married Elizabeth Dowling in 1938. After receiving his medical degree from the University of Pennsylvania in 1942, he served as a Captain in the Army Medical Corps in Europe. He died in 1963, aged fifty-one. The clinic was designed by Wright as a favor to a friend. Two other doctors, Bruce McIntyre and Whalen, had their offices here. A one-story office building, it is now occupied by the First State Bank. c96

BITTER ROOT VALLEY SITES

See map on p66 for location.

SITE OF TOWN PLAN FOR BITTER ROOT VALLEY, north of Darby, Montana
1909 0926

■ Bitter Root Valley is situated in the mountains above Darby. About a hundred miles in length, it encompasses Lake Como. Though the land is fertile, it requires irrigation to make horticulture such as apple growing viable. At the beginning of this century, the Bitter Root Valley Irrigation Company was set up in an attempt to raise $3.5 million to install a large system to irrigate the valley. Frederick D Nichols, the Vice-President and General Manager of the Como Orchards Land Company, publicized the development plans in a local promotional newspaper. In 1905, a plan was presented to the Chicagoan WI Moody. By May 1909, there were fifty-six miles of canals installed and the land company had sold 15,000 acres. By 1910, there were 2,500 acres planted with apples. Professor EP Sandsten of the Horticulture Department of the University of Wisconsin worked in the local nurseries preparing the orchards. The Illinois Chemical Company of Chicago was responsible for soil analysis and the fertilizer was prepared and sold by Armour & Company also of Chicago. There was an office for the irrigation company in the building of the First National Bank of Chicago. In February 1909, Wright visited the valley. The plans that he had drawn up for the town were widely promoted and his suggestions for the town's housing made available to the public. The town was planned just up the slope from the railroad station. The development, however, came to an abrupt end in 1913 when apple blight struck. In 1916, a Chicago bank foreclosed the company. Nevertheless the irrigation canal, which was constructed at this time, is still in use.

BITTER ROOT INN SITE, north of Darby, Montana
1909 0918

■ Designed by Wright in 1909, the inn was completed and open to customers by May 1910. It burned down in July 1924.

COMO ORCHARDS COTTAGES
469 Bunkhouse Road, University Heights
Darby, Montana 59829
1909 & 1910 0918 1002

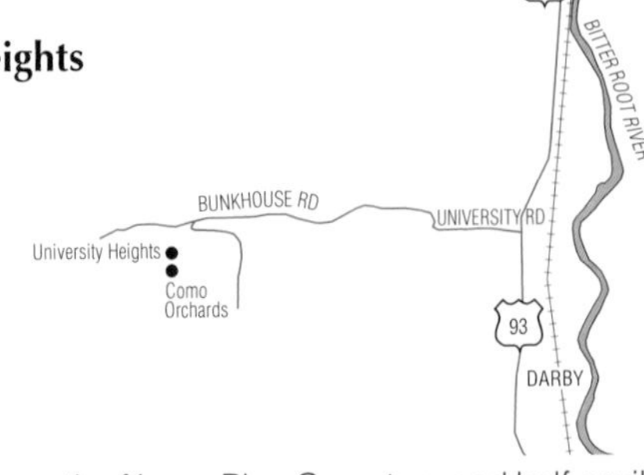

GPS: N 46 01.894
W 114 12.697
UTM: 12 T 04820 62
4948 206

Directions: Bunkhouse Road is 0.2 miles north of Lone Pine Cemetery and half a mil north of Cole Avenue on the north side of Darby. Highway 93 goes north and sout through the town. Turn west off 93 onto University Road, which turns into Bunkhouse and around the small, steep hill half a mile west of 93. Continue around to the north c the hill for 2.1 miles from 93 to the former entry drive to Como Orchards.

Accessibility: The buildings are up on a rise and cannot be approached.

■ These two cottages are all that remain of University Heights, which was designed fc the Como Orchards Land Company (see p65) to accommodate visiting academic from Northwestern University and the universities at Minnesota, Wisconsin and Chicagc In 1910, there were a dozen cabins and a clubhouse. Fifty-eight buildings were plannec The buildings varied in several ways from those in the original drawings. In 1945, th clubhouse was torn down, several of the cabins were dismantled and the lumber wa salvaged. One cabin remains in its original condition, the other has been remodeled. c9

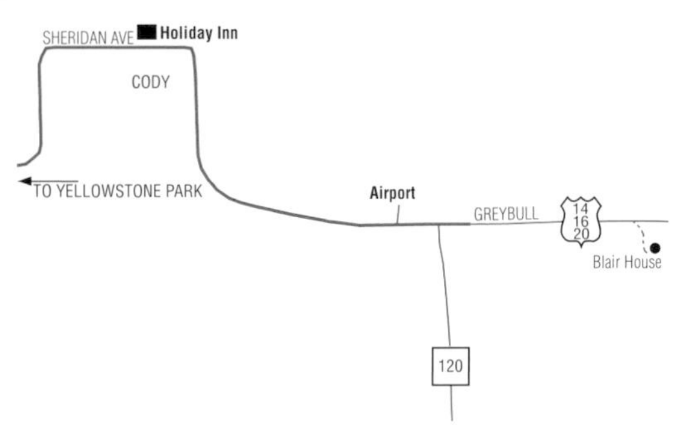

QUINTIN BLAIR HOUSE
5588 Greybull Highway
Cody, Wyoming
1952 5203

GPS: N 44 35.396
W 108 59.840
UTM: 12 T 065 8963
49 303 50

Directions: Cody is in the northwest corner of Wyoming, just east of Yellowstone National Park. The house is on the east side of Cody 1.4 miles west of the airport on Highway 14, 16, 20.

Accessibility: The house cannot be seen from the street.

■ Ruth Blair was a student of Bruce Goff while he was at the Academy of Fine Arts at the Art Institute of Chicago. In 1939, Bruce Goff, Ruth Blair and her husband Quintin visited Taliesin, where they were introduced to Wright. In conversation with them Wright suggested that he design a house for them. When they told Goff of the offer, he suggested they take Wright up on it. The Blairs had prospered through their investment in motels: they had managed and constructed several Holiday Inns in the West. Two additions were made to the original house, one designed by Goff and the other by John DeKoven Hill of Taliesin Associated Architects at Taliesin. c96

ARCHIE B TEATER STUDIO
583 River Road
Bliss, Idaho 83314
1952 5211

GPS: N 42 52.799
W 114 54.905

Directions: Bliss is just west of Interstate 84 at interchange 141 in southern Idaho about 30 miles west of Twin Falls. The first road to the south past the buildings that comprise Bliss is named Bliss Grade. Turn south onto it for 1.1 miles down a series of sharp turns to River Road. Continue south for 2.8 miles to Old Sage Road and the studio. The studio is on the river side of the road.

Accessibility: The studio is near to the road but obscured by trees during the summer.

■ Archie Teater was fifty when he wrote to Wright in October 1951, requesting a design for a small house and studio on a small outcrop of land overlooking the Snake River. His wife, Patricia, had worked with Jenkin Lloyd Jones, Wright's uncle, at the University of Chicago. After marrying Archie in 1940, Patricia started to successfully direct his artistic efforts – Teater had had a log cabin art studio in Jackson Hole since 1920. Construction was started by the fall of 1953. Wes Peters went to the site and laid it out; Tom Casey supervised the construction. By 1957, the Teaters had moved in. The present owner has restored it since it was abandoned by the Teaters in the mid-1970s. c96

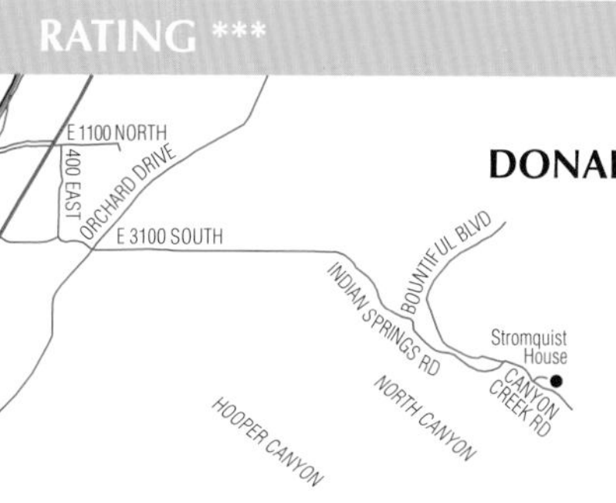

DONALD STROMQUIST HOUSE

1289 Canyon Creek Road
Bountiful, Utah 84010
1958 5626

GPS: N 40 50.802
W 111 51.057

Directions: The area immediately surrounding the house is made up of streets that vary in density as the population increases. Exit Interstate 15 at interchange 315 and drive east to 3100 South. Continue eastwards into Indian Springs Road and onto Canyon Creek Road. The house is on the north side of the street.

Accessibility: The house can be seen from the street.

The house is triangular in plan as well as in elevation. The windows are not set on the horizontal but follow the pitched roof line. This imbalance upsets the equilibrium. The house is very small, but takes advantage of the steep site and asserts its presence. The interior and exterior was recently repainted with a color chosen by Taliesin Associated Architects. c91

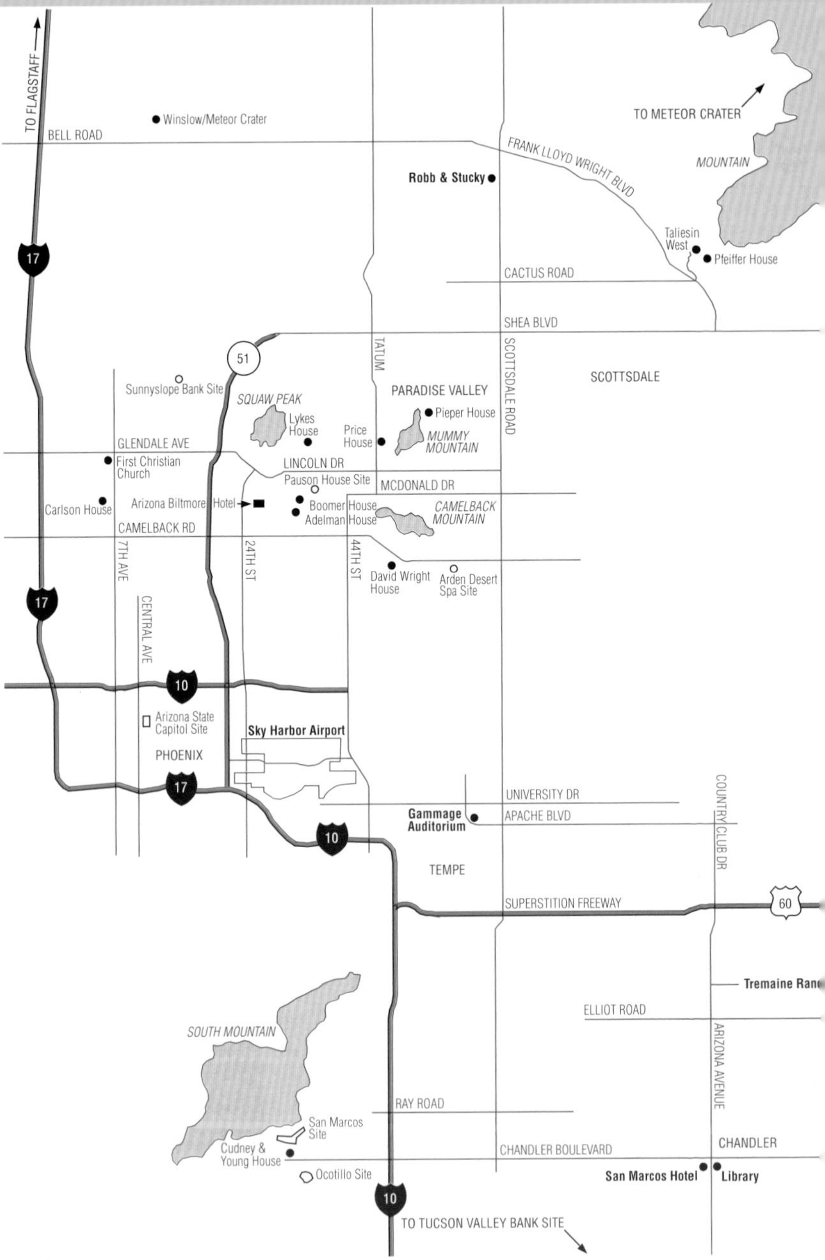

TO FLAGSTAFF
Winslow/Meteor Crater
BELL ROAD
TO METEOR CRATER
FRANK LLOYD WRIGHT BLVD
MOUNTAIN
Robb & Stucky
17
Taliesin West
Pfeiffer House
CACTUS ROAD
SHEA BLVD
51
TATUM
SCOTTSDALE ROAD
SCOTTSDALE
Sunnyslope Bank Site
SQUAW PEAK
PARADISE VALLEY
Pieper House
Lykes House
Price House
MUMMY MOUNTAIN
GLENDALE AVE
First Christian Church
LINCOLN DR
Pauson House Site
MCDONALD DR
Carlson House
Arizona Biltmore Hotel
Boomer House
Adelman House
CAMELBACK MOUNTAIN
CAMELBACK RD
7TH AVE
24TH ST
44TH ST
David Wright House
Arden Desert Spa Site
17
CENTRAL AVE
10
Arizona State Capitol Site
Sky Harbor Airport
PHOENIX
17
UNIVERSITY DR
COUNTRY CLUB DR
Gammage Auditorium
APACHE BLVD
10
TEMPE
SUPERSTITION FREEWAY
60
Tremaine Ran
ELLIOT ROAD
SOUTH MOUNTAIN
ARIZONA AVENUE
RAY ROAD
San Marcos Site
Cudney & Young House
CHANDLER BOULEVARD
CHANDLER
Ocotillo Site
San Marcos Hotel
Library
10
TO TUCSON VALLEY BANK SITE

■ Phoenix has grown rapidly but has never had the density of other major cities. Nearly all of the housing stock is made up of single family houses with minimal yards. This makes for long commutes to businesses and other services. A photo taken in 1940 shows no buildings whatever between Taliesin and Squaw Peak Mountain. Wright's designs for this area began in the 1920s and spanned over thirty years. The project that first brought him to this area was assisting in the construction details of the Arizona Biltmore Hotel (p74) for Albert Chase McArthur (1881-1951), the architect son of a much earlier client, Warren McArthur (see MetroChicago volume). As with many of Wright's clients, Dr Alexander Chandler learned about this work and hired Wright for the design of his hotel and resort (p83).

An interesting Wright design in the vicinity of Phoenix, which might be worth a detour, is the Meteor Crater Inn (Opus #4822); it was planned for the meteor crater to the east of Flagstaff, near Winslow. The crater is 500 feet deep and a mile across with a visitor's center on the northwest rim. It has become an increasinly popular tourist attraction since movies, such as *Armageddon* and *Deep Impact*, started featuring deep craters created by extraterrestial objects. Burton Tremaine, who operated the crater as a privately owned enterprise, commissioned the inn. Originally from Connecticut, Tremaine set up a foundation there and was an avid collector of modern art. In 1988 and 1991, most of his collection was auctioned off at Christie's. His brother lived in a 1947 Richard Neutra-designed house in Montecito, California.

FIRST CHRISTIAN CHURCH (SOUTHWEST CHRISTIAN SEMINARY)

6750 North 7th Avenue
Phoenix, Arizona 80513
1950 5033

GPS: N 33 32.073
W 112 04.992

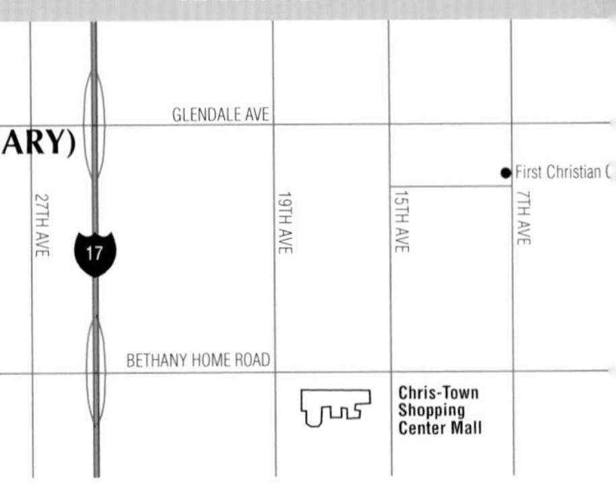

Directions: The church is east of Interstate 17, just two blocks south of Glendale Avenue on 7th Avenue. It is on the west side of 7th.

Accessibility: The church can be seen from the street. There are regular services and guided tours can be made by reservation.

■ This seminary for the First Christian Church was designed at the end of Wright's life and constructed after he died. It differs from the original drawings in several respects, mostly due to budgetry constraints. Consequently, some architectural historians have objected to it being included in his oeuvre.

Wright drew up this design in 1950 for Dr Canary Peyton. In October 1952, Dr William Boice founded a congregation with thirty-four people, called the Southwest Christian Seminary. By 1966, the First Christian Church contacted Olgivanna Wright to inquire about adapting the original design for the Seminary. The EJ Wasielewski Construction Company began work in May 1971. By 1973 the 28,400-square-feet sanctuary was completed at a cost of $1,200,000. A122-foot-tall bell tower was added in 1978. c96

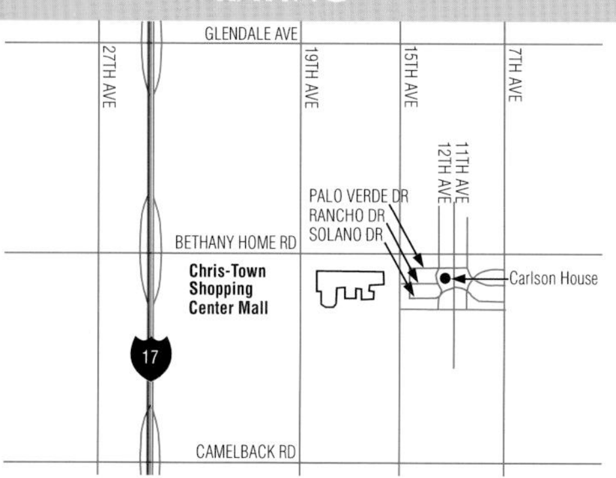

RAYMOND CARLSON HOUSE
1123 West Palo Verde Drive
Phoenix, Arizona 85013
1950 5004

GPS: N 33 31.385
W 112 04.992

Directions: The house is east of Interstate 17, just south of Bethany Home Road. Turn south from Bethany onto 12th Avenue one block. The house is on the southeast corner.

Accessibility: The house is now obscured by the lot line plantings.

■ Raymond Carlson was born in1906, in Leadville, Colorado, the son of a miner who came to Arizona due to his ill health. In 1929, Carlson graduated from Stanford University with Phi Beta Kappa. During the depression, Carlson did odd jobs until he got a position with the State Highway Department. Once in the department, he became editor of *Arizona Highways*. He reoriented the magazine away from technical information about Arizona's roads and started extolling the natural features and activities of the state. Many of the issues featured Wright's Arizona work. Carlson remained editor, with the exception of a stint in the army, until his retirement in 1971.

The Carlson House has one of the most interesting, inexpensive approaches to construction. It is based on a grid of 4 by 4 wood posts and Masonite infill panels. In some parts of the house clearances are tight, but the overall design is delightful. c94

ARIZONA BILTMORE HOTEL
2701 East Arizona Biltmore Circle
Phoenix, Arizona 85016
1927 2710

GPS: N 33 31.349
W 112 01.365

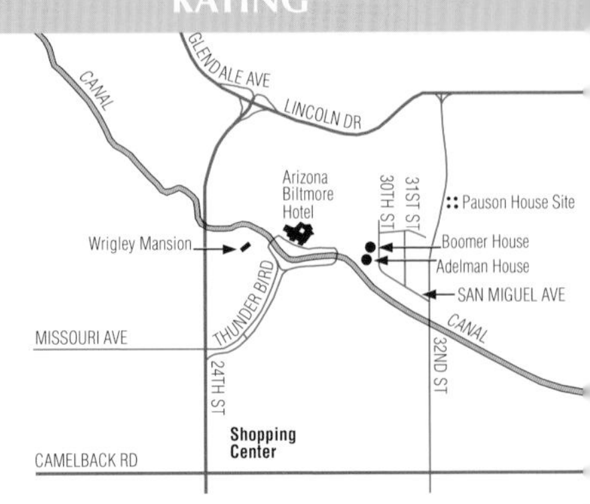

Directions: Halfway between Bethany Home Road (see p73) to the north and Camelback Road on the south is Missouri Avenue. At the intersection of Missouri and 24th Street is the entry road to the Biltmore property. Follow this road to the east as it turns to the north and back easterly. Cross the small bridge to the hotel.

Accessibility: The hotel is always accessible.

■ The architect of the hotel was Albert McArthur (1881-1951), the son of Warren McArthur, one of Wright's clients dating back to the 1890s (see MetroChicago volume). Albert had himself worked for Wright, in Oak Park, and again, briefly, at Taliesin, before moving to Arizona to be with his brothers. His two brothers Charles H and Warren McArthur Jr had gone out to Phoenix in 1910 – two years before Arizona became a state. They were successful automobile dealers, in alliance with the financiers the Los Angeles Biltmore Company. The site that the brothers acquired for the hotel was a 621-acre plot with about 200 acres allotted to the hotel.

After reading about the success of the California block system Wright had used in several Los Angeles houses, Albert McArthur wrote to Wright asking for permission to use it in the design for the Arizona Biltmore. Wright went to Phoenix in early 1928 and stayed until May to help McArthur develop the use of the blocks in his design. The designer of the face of the individual block was Emry Kopta, a local sculptor. The blocks were made of dry mixed concrete, using the same process employed in the Storer, Ennis and Millard Houses (pp53, 55 and 61 respectively), all designed in the mid twenties for Southern California.

The hotel was officially opened on 23 February 1929. Both the hotel and fifteen guest cottages were ready for occupancy, after only six months in construction. The hotel, however, ran into difficulties and was taken over by William Wrigley. Since its initial construction there have been several additions. Most of them were designed by Taliesin Associated Architects, the successor firm to Wright's practice. c79 & 85.

JORGINE BOOMER HOUSE
5808 North 30th Street
Phoenix, Arizona 85016
1953 5302 5305

GPS: N 33 31.367
W 12 01.016

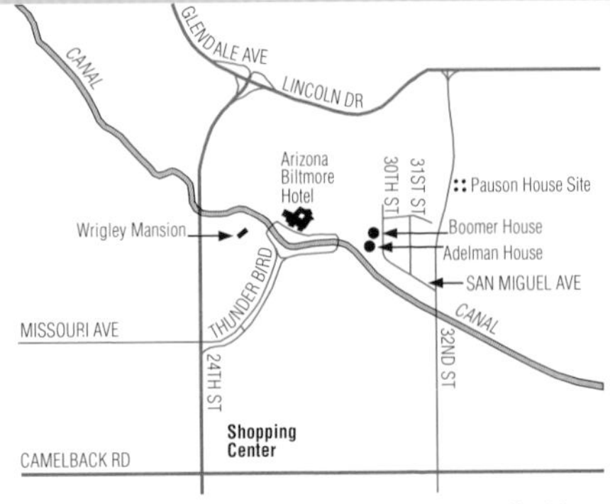

Directions: The house is between Lincoln Drive and Camelback Road. Turn off either street onto 32nd Street. Take a west turning just north of the canal bridge at the traffic light at San Miguel Avenue and go up and over the hill to 30th Street. The house is the second after the bend on the west side of the street, just north of the Adelman House.

Accessibility: The house is hidden behind dense foliage.

■ The house was commissioned by Norwegian-born Jorgine Boomer (nee Slettede), the widow of Lucius Boomer, who owned the Waldorf-Astoria Hotel in New York. It is one of the most unusual of Wright's later works. Based on a triangle, like the Clark House at Carmel (p38), its diagonals extend into the elevations. Its roof overhangs make it appear much larger than its small floor area. The orientation of the building is to the northeast, minimizing southwest exposure to the hot sun and giving it exceptional views of Squaw Peak.

The house was Jorgine Boomer's second attempt to build a Wright house. In April 1945, she tried to remodel the Pauson House (Opus #4707, see p78 for original house) – but the cost was estimated at $35,000. c81

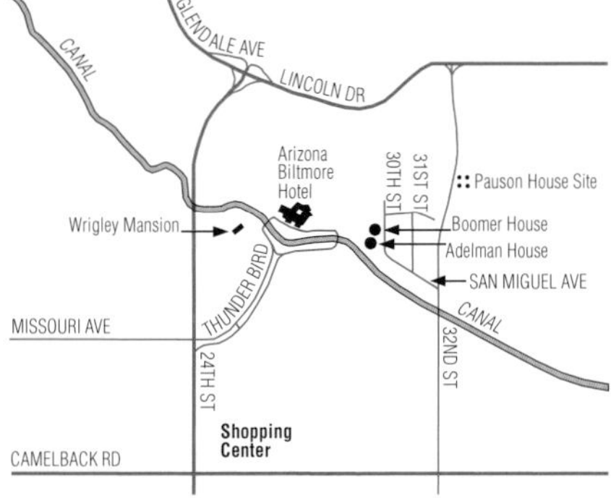

BENJAMIN ADELMAN HOUSE
5802 North 30th Street
Phoenix, Arizona 85016
1951 5101

GPS: N 33 31.303
W 12 01.010

Directions: The house is between Lincoln Drive and Camelback Road. Turn off either street onto 32nd Street. Take a west turning just north of the canal bridge at the traffic light at San Miguel Avenue and go up and over the hill to 30th Street. The house is after the bend on the west side of the street, just south of the Boomer House.

Accessibility: The house can be seen from the street.

■ Benjamin Adelman owned a successful laundry in Milwaukee. In the 1940s, Wright executed an unrealized design for it (Opus #4507). This was Adelman's winter home; he met up with friends at the Biltmore to play cards. The house, built by local Indians, is divided in two distinct parts: the main block containing the living and dining areas, kitchen and master suite; and the rear north wing containing three guest rooms and two bathrooms. The original construction cost $25,000. The two volumes were connected by extensions of the block walls, which also defined a small grass yard. Unfortunately, recent additions have almost obliterated the original Wright design. Wright also executed a house for Adelman's son Albert (Opus #4801 and #4834). c79

PHOENIX AREA SITES

See maps on pp70-71 for locations.

ELIZABETH ARDEN DESERT SPA SITE, Sunlight, Phoenix, Arizona 1945 4506

■ This scheme was designed for Elizabeth Arden, the cosmetic manufacturer, as a winter spa. It was to be located near Camelback Mountain, which is shown in the rendering. The project was put on hold because of the scarcity of building materials and labor at the end of the war.

ARIZONA STATE CAPITOL SITE, Central Avenue, Phoenix, Arizona 1957 5732

■ This was Wright's alternative, unsolicited scheme for a New State Capitol Building, publicized by Lloyd Clark, a reporter on the *Phoenix Gazette*.

DONAHOE TRIPTYCH SITE, Paradise Valley, Phoenix, Arizona 1959 5901

■ This design was for a winter home on a plot of land Helen Donahoe bought on the top of a mountain, which was to be connected with two other mountain tops by bridges. The designs were drawn just before Wright's death on 9 April 1959.

ROSE PAUSON HOUSE SITE, 5859 31st Street (formerly Orange Road), Phoenix, Arizona 85016 1940 4011

■ The Pauson House was damaged by fire in 1942, just two years after it was built. All of the wood portion burned away and the stone masses remained. Wright described it as a 'magnificent ruin.' The house was intended to be a winter retreat for Rose Pauson, an artist, who lived in Pacific Heights, San Francisco. The City of Phoenix preferred to give up their Federal money for this part of the 32nd Street improvement scheme rather than fight the preservationists who opposed the demolition of the house's remaining stonework. This land was a part of the original Biltmore property.

VALLEY NATIONAL BANK SITES, Tucson and Sunnyslope, Arizona 1947 4722 and 1948 4734

■ Walter Reed Bimson commissioned these designs for two branches of the Valley National Bank in 1947-48. Bimson was born in 1892 and attended the University of Chicago, before entering the Navy, which he served in until 1918. Between 1920 and 1933, he was a banker at the Harris Bank in Chicago. He then moved to Arizona and the Valley National Bank, becoming Chairman of the Board in 1953.

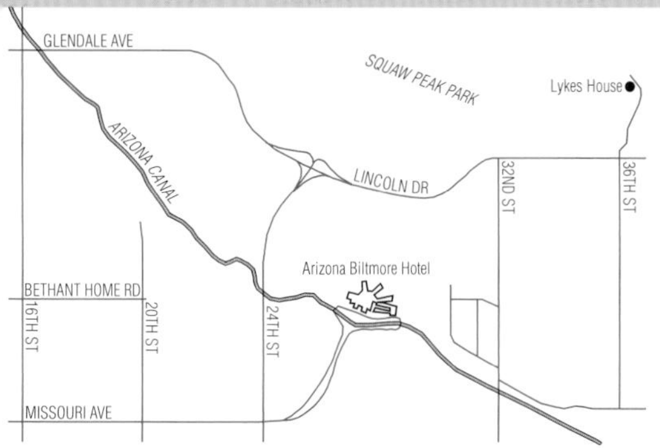

NORMAN LYKES HOUSE

6636 North 36th Street
Phoenix, Arizona 85018
1966 5908

GPS: N 33 32.317
W 112 00.133

Directions: East of 24th Street, Glendale Avenue becomes Lincoln Drive. Take 36th Street north of Lincoln to the house, which is on the west side of the street up the hill.

Accessibility: The house can be seen from the road.

■ Norman Lykes was left an inheritance by his family in Florida. When he married his wife Aimee, who was from the North, they compromised between the North and the South by deciding to live in the West. In 1953, they moved to Scottsdale. Through a friend with a dog that ran off to Taliesin, Lykes met Olgivanna Wright and became acquainted with John Rattenbury. Aimee Lykes was first enamored by the Robie House while a student at the University of Chicago. The Lykeses contacted Wright for a house design and had sketches drawn up in 1959, just before Wright's death. Rattenbury developed the sketches into working drawings and construction was completed by 1967 on the original site. c96

DAVID WRIGHT HOUSE
5212 Exeter Boulevard
Phoenix, Arizona
1950 5030

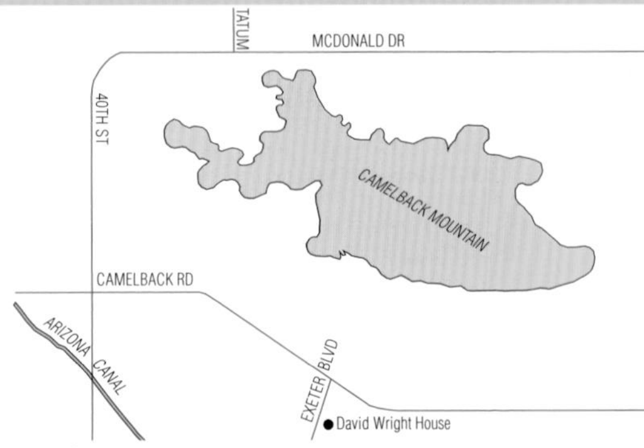

GPS: N 33 30 51
W 111 57 40

Directions: The house is on the south side of Exeter and about half a mile south of Camelback Road.

Accessibility: The house cannot be seen from the street.

■ David Samuel Wright (1906-97) was the third son and fifth child of Wright and Catherine Tobin Wright. He was born in the Wright House and Studio in Oak Park (see MetroChicago volume). Through his work he was associated with the Portland Cement Association in Chicago and Skokie, Illinois. He became a sales representative of a concrete block company and eventually moved to Phoenix, where he asked his father to design a house for him. Wright proposed 'The House on the Desert' design. Jack Howe's famous color-pencil perspective and plan illustrate the radical solution that included raising the living quarters above the grade to make it more accessible to desert breezes. Wright also specially designed the house a rug (Opus #5121). This has the richness of any fine Persian carpet.

A guesthouse (Opus #5431) was built several years after the main house. c77

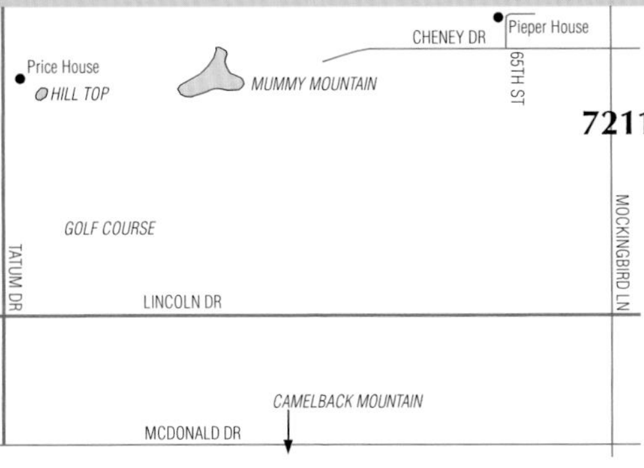

HAROLD PRICE SR HOUSE
7211 North Tatum, Paradise Valley
Phoenix, Arizona 85253
1954 5419

GPS: N33 32.317
W 112 00.133

Directions: The house is on the west side of Tatum Drive across from the golf course about half a mile north of Lincoln Drive and south of Shea Boulevard.

Accessibility: The house can be seen from the street and from the vacant property both north and south of the house.

■ This was the winter home of Harold Price Sr, who was responsible for the Price Tower (p92). An unusual house, its design was thoroughly adapted to the desert climate. It contains a large room with an opening in the roof, similar to the 1921 design Wright executed for himself entitled a 'Desert Dwelling.' This roof is held up off the walls by steel piping, which allow breezes to flow through the gap between the roof and the walls. The house incorporates wood panels with designs by Eugene Masselink painted on them. The concrete block is more typical of the 8 by 8 by 16 standard block that is generally available in contractor supply houses. It is not the customized block that was used in the Usonian Automatic Houses, such as the Pieper House (p82). Wright designed a house for Harold Price Jr in Bartlesville, Oklahoma (p93). c94

ARTHUR PIEPER HOUSE
6442 East Cheney Road, Paradise Valley
Phoenix, Arizona 85253
1952 5218

GPS: N 33 32.961
W 111 56.475

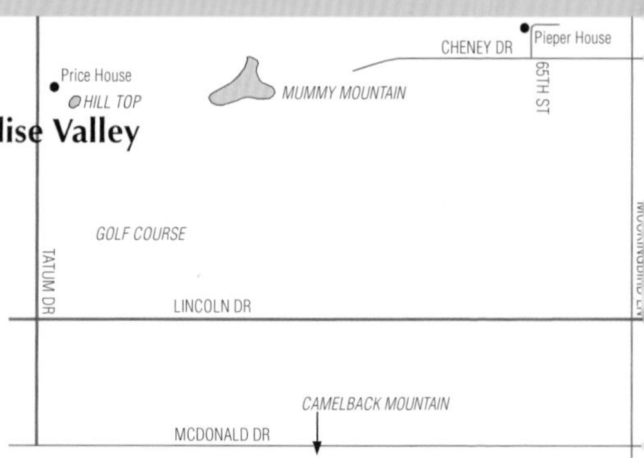

Directions: From Lincoln Drive take Mockingbird Lane, which runs north–south, east of Tatum Drive, for a mile north before turning off to Cheney Drive. Once on Cheney look out for the right turning to 65th Street. The house is the third from the corner on the west side of the street. The address is on Cheney but the entry is on 65th. The remnants of the house are behind the new construction.

Accessibility: The house cannot be seen from the street.

■ The Pieper House was spoiled by a new house in 1996 that was built in front of and attached to the original Wright building. Pieper was married to, and later divorced from, Iovanna Wright, the daughter of Wright and Olgivanna. He was, for a time, in partnership with the architect Charles Montooth. The Usonian Automatic House was very small and was located to the north of two other Montooth designs that are often confused with the Wright design. c96

CHANDLER SITES

Chandler is about 20 miles south and just east of Phoenix. See map on pp70-71 for locations.

OCOTILLO CAMP SITE, south of Chandler Boulevard, Chandler, Arizona 1928 2702

■ The site is now a dull housing development and there are no signs of the original camp. It was built just to the south of the San Marcos in the Desert site to accommodate those working on the proposed hotel – Wright had six assistants engaged on it including his son Lloyd. It was composed of wood structures that had canvas roofs. The buildings were only extant from January until May of 1929. The camp was burned in a fire, but evidence of its existence was visible until quite recently.

SAN MARCOS IN THE DESERT SITE, north of Chandler Boulevard, Chandler, Arizona 1928 2704

■ In 1887, Dr Alexander Chandler (1859-1950) came to the Phoenix area from Detroit as the Territorial Veterinarian for the Cattle Sanitary Board. At that time, the area around Chandler was rich alfalfa land fed by the Salt River. In 1892, Chandler resigned his position and took up land development full time. He bought 20,000 acres and installed irrigation canals. His funding came in part from DM Ferry of Detroit's Ferry Seed Company – the same Ferry family that Avery Coonley married into when he wed Queenie Ferry (see Coonley House, MetroChicago volume). On 17 May 1912, he founded the Town of Chandler. In 1913, he built a San Marcos Hotel for the center of the town – now operated by Sheraton. He promoted the land sale to those in California and sold $50,000 worth on opening day.

Chandler held the land for San Marcos in the Desert for over ten years before getting Wright to design the hotel for him in early 1928, when he was working on the construction of the Arizona Biltmore in Phoenix. It was to be the largest project Wright had undertaken since the Imperial Hotel, Tokyo (p130). The project was halted by the Stock Market Crash of October 1929. Paul Mueller formerly of Adler & Sullivan's office was all ready to begin construction. In 1930, and as late as June 1931, work on the scheme was not completely over, although by 1934 Chandler had lost the property. Wright also executed designs for a Chandler Block House and Camp Cabins (Opus #2708 and #2804 respectively).

CUDNEY AND YOUNG HOUSE SITES, Chandler, Arizona 1927 2707 and 2707

■ The first house was for Owen D Young (1874-1962) and introduced a diagonal or diamond block variation used in the other San Marcos buildings. Young was a patent attorney for General Electric in 1913 and became Chairman of the Board for GE by 1922. He founded and became Chairman of the Boards for both RCA and NBC. Young was on the GE Board at the same time as Burton Tremaine (Meteor Crater Opus #4822, p71) and visited his ranch north of Chandler, where he met Wright. Ralph and Wellington Cudney's house was on an adjacent parcel. They were brothers from New York and Connecticut and were financiers.

GRADY GAMMAGE MEMORIAL AUDITORIUM

Apache Boulevard
Tempe, Arizona 85281
1959 5904

GPS: N 33 24.969
W 111 56.236

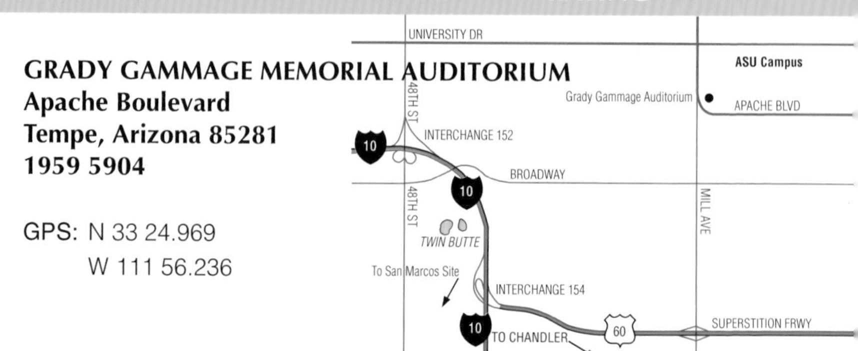

Directions: Drive south on Scottsdale Road, which changes its name at the Arizona State University campus to Rural Road (to the east of the map, parallel with Mill Avenue). From Rural Road, the auditorium is half a mile west on Apache Boulevard just where the street turns to the north into Mill Avenue. It is on the northeast of Apache. The auditorium is at the southwest corner of the campus.

Accessibility: The building is open during scheduled performances.

■ Wright designed but did not oversee the construction of the auditorium. He died in April 1959 and the formal commission did not come from the Board of Regents until June, with the initial contract dated 30 April 1960. Like the Marin County Civic Center (p25), the design of the building was simplified during construction. After Wright's death, Wes Peters headed the project. The acoustics of the auditorium are, however, well known for their high quality. The balcony, the Grand Tier, is detached from the back wall, which releases sound energy that would otherwise be trapped under the balcony.

The auditorium opened with an inaugural concert in September 1964. c77

TALIESIN WEST
12621 Frank Lloyd Wright Boulevard
Scottsdale, Arizona 85261
1938 3803

GPS: N 33 36.419
W 111 50.804

Directions: Taliesin West is in far northeast Scottsdale at the base of the mountains. It is north of Shea Boulevard and east of Scottsdale Road (see map on p70). Take Scottsdale north to Cactus Road and drive east to and across (at about 114th Street) Frank Lloyd Wright Boulevard, up and over the canal keeping to the left and on to the parking lot.

Accessibility: Tours are given every day except for the four major holidays and are made by reservation. Call 602/860-2700. There are several tour options to choose from. They are well worth the admission price.

■ For the sake of his health, it was recommended by his doctor that Wright escape the cold and damp Wisconsin winters. Having become familiar with the Phoenix area through the Biltmore and San Marcos projects (pp74-75 and p83), in 1937 he bought about 600 acres northeast of downtown Phoenix at the base of the McDowell Mountains. By 1940, the initial construction work at Taliesin West was complete. The building work was done by apprentices, who laid the stones in a new way, setting the blocks into tapered wood forms with the faces on the outside. Wright and his apprentices had a long winter semester

here as they celebrated Easter in Arizona with the cacti in bloom, before returning to Wisconsin for the summer and Wright's Birthday on 8 June. The original roofs to the drafting studios and bedrooms were canvas, like those at Ocotillo (p83). The large 'bents' or trusses were originally redwood. The joint between the redwood and the canvas was not watertight: water was allowed into the buildings and directed out through small gutters. After his death, the Taliesin Fellowship decided to spend more time at 'camp,' and replaced the canvas and redwood with steel and insulated fiberglass to retain the air conditioning that was then introduced. As with his Oak Park Studio and Taliesin, the building was continuously being added to and changed. Unlike Taliesin in Wisconsin and Ocotillo, there was never a major fire.

The area around Taliesin West has been spoiled by the intrusion of electrical high-tension wires and a canal that crosses the property at the southern border. Originally the track was undefined and cars drove cross country, avoiding the Saguaro cactus and the sharp spines of the *cholla*. Once Shea Boulevard had been laid, one turned off north onto a long straight road leading to a wonderful serpentine road, remnants of which are still used. There was a small red marker at Shea with an arrow indicating 'to Taliesin' (Opus #5301), although it was never hard to see the camp buildings up the slope. That view has also now been obliterated by the subdivisions that crowd the entry.

This is now the headquarters of the Frank Lloyd Wright Foundation and the Frank Lloyd Wright School of Architecture. The archives that include Wright's letters and drawings are located in a new study center. The Director of Archives, Bruce Brooks Pfeiffer's father, is responsible for the Arthur Pfeiffer House at Taliesin West. Built in 1971-72, it realizes Wright's unbuilt design for Ralph Jester (Opus #3807), who commissioned the drawings for a site at Palos Verde, California. Olgivanna Lloyd Wright suggested the change in scale. The major rooms are separate structures all joined by a common roof. c77&79

COLORADO SITES

ESTES PARK
BOULDER
DENVER
COLORADO

HORSESHOE INN, Estes Park, Colorado
1908 0814

■ Though there is no evidence that Wright's design was ever built, Willard Ashton did construct an inn on North Road in the Rocky Mountain National Park, which was no longer extant in 1931.

The year following the design of the inn, Mamah Cheney left nearby Boulder, in Colorado, abandoning her children and husband, to meet Wright in New York for their two-year sojourn in Paris.

HOUSE ON THE MESA, Denver, Colorado
1931 3102

■ The site is fictional, but was probably based on what is now known as Cramer Park in Mountain View. According to Bob Sweeney, it was designed for George (1884-1975) and Jean (1886-1974) Cramer of Denver. The house was perhaps the longest Wright ever designed at 360 feet, compared to the Ennis House in Los Angeles at 250 feet (p55). It was for a family with four children, two maids and a chauffeur.

Pfeiffer House, Taliesin West, built 1971-72 to Wright's 1938 design.

ARNOLD FRIEDMAN (FIR TREE) HOUSE
Highway 63
Pecos, New Mexico 87552
1945 4512, gatehouse 1952 5224

GPS: 35 37.886
105 40.827

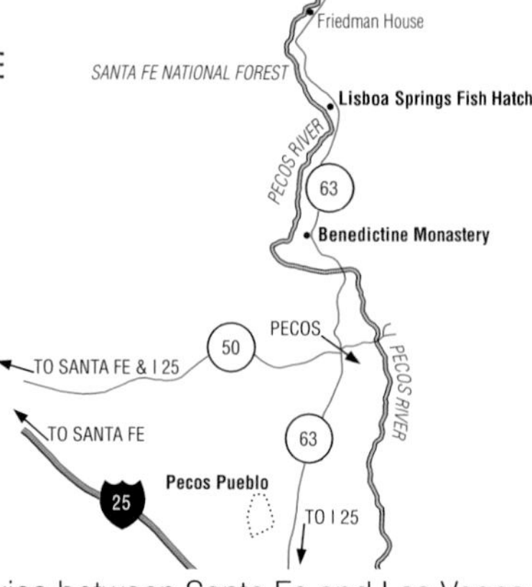

Directions: Pecos is in north-central New Mexico between Santa Fe and Las Vegas, just north of Interstate 25, between exits 299 (Route 50) and 307 (Route 63). From the intersection of 50 and 63 drive north on 63 for 4.6 miles to the entry drive.

Accessibility: The house cannot be seen from the street. It is guarded by dogs.

■ Born in 1900 in Plumerville, Arkansas, Arnold Friedman graduated from Columbia University in 1922. In 1925, he and Godfrey Lebhar made their publishing debut with *Chain Store Age,* which he followed up with many other successful publications. During the 1940s, Friedman lived in the New York City suburb of Great Neck while Ben Rebhuhn was constructing his Wright-designed house (Opus #3801). The Pecos House was a summer house and had no heating. Its was to cost no more than $10,000. WA Stanton of Santa Fe was the contractor. The house is now the center of operations for a cattle ranch. Every year, Friedman used to send Wright smoked turkey for Christmas. c58

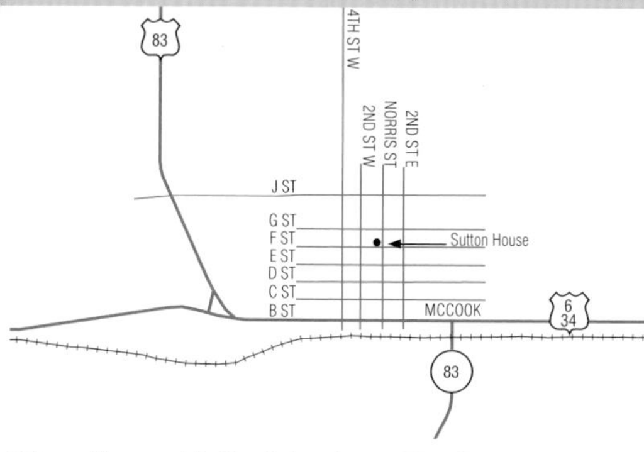

HARVEY P SUTTON HOUSE
602 Norris Avenue
McCook, Nebraska 69001
1907 0710 (0516, 0525)

GPS: N 40 12.157
W 100 37.559

Directions: McCook is about 65 miles south of Interstate 80, along Highway 83. At Highway 6/34, drive east for a mile to Norris Street and turn north for four blocks or 0.3 miles to F Street. The house is on the corner.

Accessibility: The house can be seen from both streets.

■ When Harvey Sutton found himself in ill health working for a musical organization in Chicago, he flipped a coin to see if he should go east or west. He decided to go west. While living in Ainsworth, Nebraska, he married Elizabeth Munson in 1886. He relocated to McCook to lead the prestigious Burlington Railroad band. Once in McCook, Sutton followed his brother Benjamin, who had a successful business in Dexter, into the jewelry trade. It was Elizabeth, rather than Harvey Sutton, who was most involved in the design and construction of the Wright house. Since the Sutton's sold it, the house has been converted into medical offices. A concrete block wall has been put up around the perimeter of the property, incorporating cherubs holding water fountains. c96

JUVENILE CULTURAL CENTER
(now Corbin Educational Center)
Yale Avenue at 21st street
between Yale and Roosevelt
Wichita, Kansas 67208
1957 5708, 5743

GPS: N 37 43.291
W 97 17.590

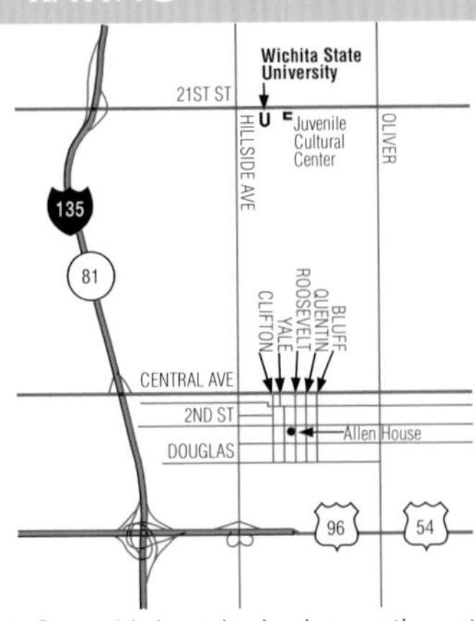

Directions: The center is on the campus of Wichita State University in the northeast section of Wichita. Exit Highway 96 at Hillside Avenue north for 1.4 miles to 21st Street and turn east for 0.3 miles. The center is on 21st Street just east of the stadium, on the south side of the street.

Accessibility: The center is visible from all sides at all times.

■ The commission of this million-dollar educational building was overseen by Jackson O Powell who held an administrative position at the center. In 1957, the Dean, Harry F Corbin, and Powell visited Wright at Taliesin to discuss the project, which had been approved by the Regents of the University. The drawings arrived in 1958. Budgetry constraints, however, meant only half of the building was completed. The entire complex was finished in 1964 when the University had only 6,000 students. The building is now used as an administrative center rather than as a classroom building. c96

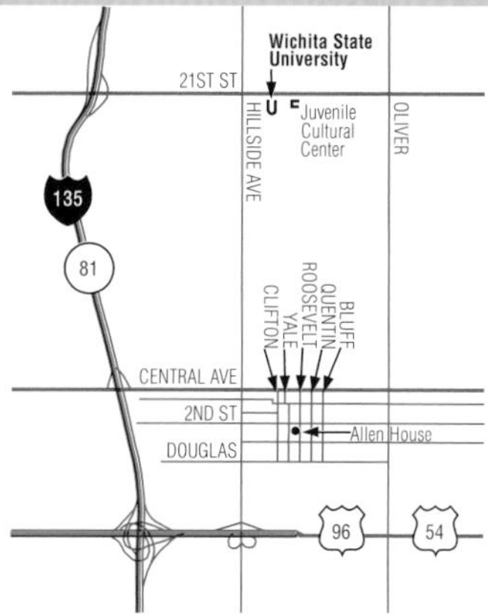

HENRY J ALLEN HOUSE
255 North Roosevelt Boulevard
Wichita, Kansas 67208
1917 1701

GPS: N 37 41.386
W 97 17.517

Directions: The Allen House is two miles exactly south of the Corbin Center. It is 0.3 miles east of Hillside at the southwest corner of Roosevelt Boulevard and 2nd Street. It is northeast of the interchange of Interstate 135 and Highway 54.

Accessibility: The house can be seen from the street.

■ Born in 1868, in Pennsylvania, Henry Allen was the successful newspaper publisher of the *Wichita Beacon*. Between 1918 and 1922, he was Governor of Kansas. One of his best friends was the newspaper publisher and political activist William Allen White, for whom Wright did some drawings for a minor house remodeling in Emporia, Kansas (Opus #1610). White introduced Allen to Wright; he was a close friend of another Wright client, Chauncey Williams of River Forest (see MetroChicago volume). Both Allen and White served as Red Cross officers in World War I; White wrote about it in *The Martial Adventures of Henry and Me* (1918). Allen died in 1950, leaving an estate of over $2,500,000. c96

PRICE TOWER
(Now Phillips 66 Petroleum)
NE 6th Street
at Dewey Avenue
Bartlesville, Oklahoma 74003
1952 5215

GPS: N 36 44.864
W 95 58.561

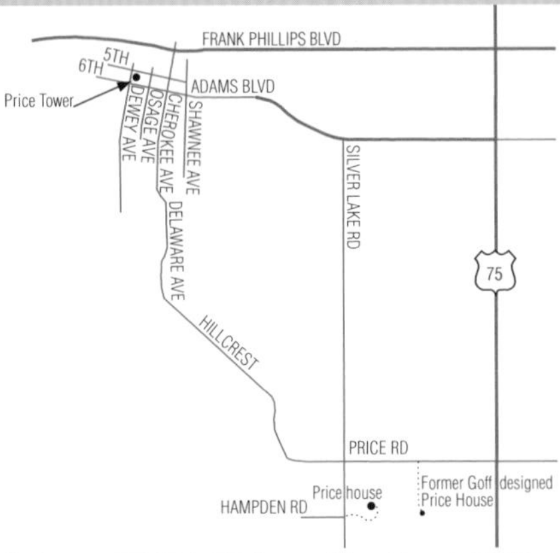

Directions: Bartlesville is 2 miles west of Highway 75. Exit 75 from either Frank Phillips Boulevard or Adams Boulevard to Dewey Avenue.

Accessibility: Access to the interior is at the time of writing undetermined.

■ The design originates from Buckminster Fuller's idea of hanging the floors of a tower from a central stem. Wright first developed the concept, in 1929, for an apartment tower for St Mark's in the Bowerie, New York City (Opus #2905 see East volume). The apartments in the Price Tower have double-story living rooms and feel spacious despite their small floor areas. Cast-aluminum chairs and tables were specially designed for the building.

Though the tower has most recently been owned by Phillips 66 Petroleum Company, the intention is now to make it the region's cultural center. The former chairman of Phillips 66 is heading an ongoing campaign to renovate and preserve the tower. c96

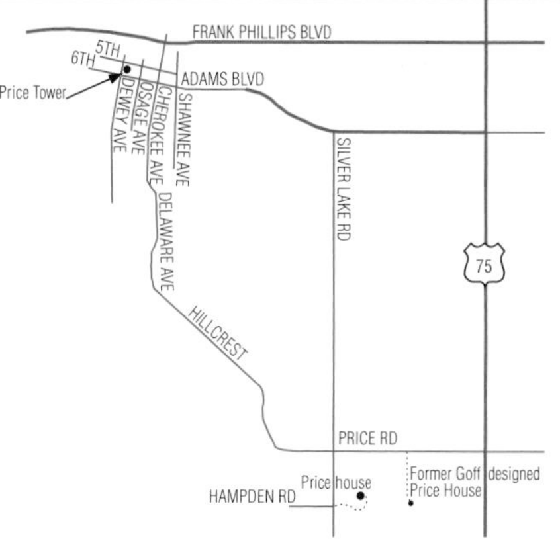

HAROLD PRICE JR HOUSE
2800 South Silver Lake Road
Bartlesville, Oklahoma 74003
1954 5421

GPS: 36 42.522
95 57.223

Directions: The house is south of Bartlesville and a mile west of Highway 75. Exit 75 at Price Road to the west. Turn off at Silver Lake Road and turn south. The gated drive is 0.4 miles south of Price Road on the east side of the street across from Hampden Road.

Accessibility: The house cannot be viewed from the road. The property is private.

■ This house has a great site on a rise from a pond facing the southwest. Its most unusual feature is the raised brick patio, cantilevered from below. It is contrary to most of Wright's preaching on the nature of materials: brick should not be used to cantilever like stone or wood, as it necessitates the sort of hidden steel supports present here.

The house was designed for Harold Price Sr's son Harold. Price Sr was a self-made man. He started out as a welder in the 1920s. By the fifties his business was one of the largest pipeline construction companies in the US. His other son, Joe, photographed the construction of the Tower for Wright's book, *The Story of the Tower* (1956). c96

RICHARD LLOYD JONES HOUSE
3704 South Birmingham Avenue
Tulsa, Oklahoma 74105
1929 2902

GPS: N 36 06.555
W 95 57.157

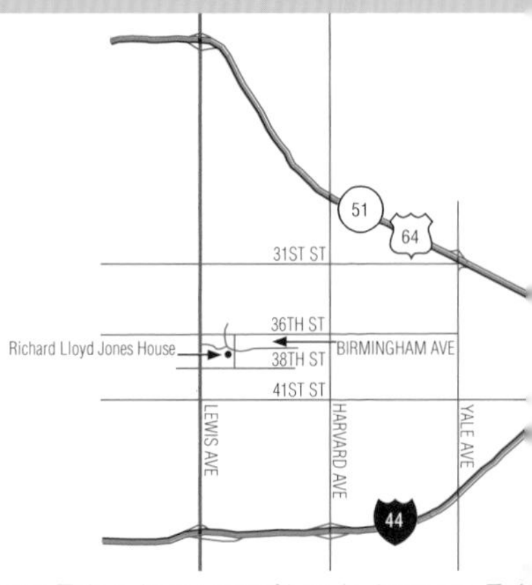

Directions: The house is southwest of downtown Tulsa, just east of Lewis Avenue. Exi Interstate 44 to the south or Highway 51 on the north to Lewis. Drive to 36th Street anc turn east 0.2 miles to Birmingham Avenue and drive south one block. The house is or the southwest corner of 37th and Birmingham.

Accessibility: The house can be seen from the street.

■ This house was built for Wright's cousin Richard Lloyd Jones (*c*1873-1963), a successfu editor who worked on *Cosmopolitan, Madison State Journal* and the *Tulsa Tribune*. Jones was also a prime mover behind the preservation of President Lincoln's birthplace ir Hodgenville, Kentucky. The first scheme for the house was lozenge shaped (Opus #2901) In 1929, Wright revised it so that it was rectangular. The contractor was Paul Mueller, whc was engaged to work on San Marcos in the Desert (p83). This is the first Wright house Bruce Goff saw; he befriended Mueller, and both Wright and his son Lloyd. c96

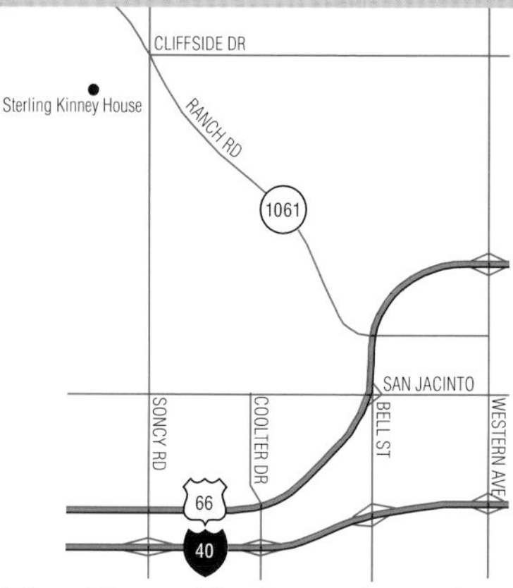

STERLING KINNEY HOUSE

Tascosa Road
Amarillo, Texas 79606
1957 5717

GPS: N 35 15.099
W 101 56.413

Directions: The house is northwest of Amarillo city center. Exit Interstate 40 at interchange 64 and take Soncy Road north for 4.3 miles to the intersection of Ranch Road (Route 1061), which becomes Tascosa Road at that interchange. The drive is about 400 feet past the intersection on the south side of the street.

Accessibility: The House is about a third of a mile down a private drive .

■ Dorothy Ann Kinney, who like her husband was an attorney, sat at the drafting board and watched her house being designed by Wright. This is the only known instance of a client witnessing the creative process. The original budget was for $35,000, not including the furniture and fixtures. By the time construction began the cost had risen to $60,000. When they wrote to Wright in 1955, the Kinneys, who had two daughters, specified that they wanted plenty of room for a large number of books and a quiet place for them to study. c86

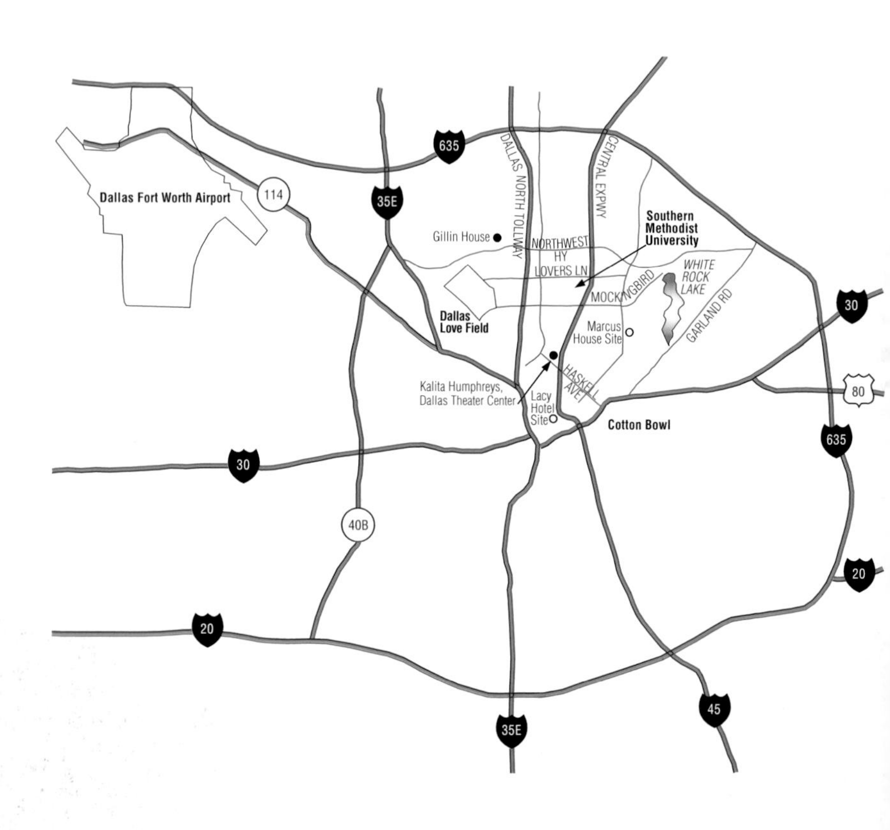

■ Until Mexico gained independence in 1821, Texas was a part of Spain. Afterwards those such as Stephen Austin, Sam Houston and Davey Crockett, fought for independence from Mexico. It was a republic for only nine years before its annexation by the US in 1845. Though Houston is now the largest city in Texas, Dallas surpasses it as a megalopolis with Fort Worth and Arlington. Dallas was founded in 1845, but only really developed with the railroads in the 1870s. During the 1930s, the city experienced its second boom when oil was discovered and made many of its citizens very wealthy.

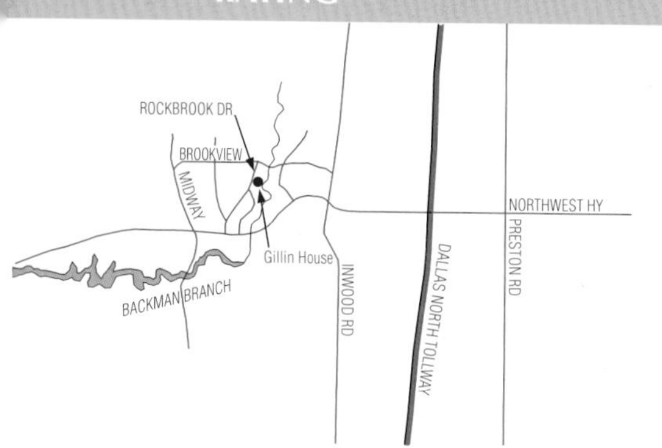

JOHN A GILLIN HOUSE
9400 Rockbrook Drive
Dallas, Texas 75220
1950 5034

GPS: N 32 52.115
W 96 49.867

Directions: There are exits from both Interstate 35E and Dallas North Tollway onto Northwest Highway. Drive from Inwood Road north one block to Brookview and go west over the little bridge to Rockbrook Drive. The house's site is on the southeast corner of Rockbrook and Brookview.

Accessibility: The house can be seen from the street through the gate.

■ John Gillin was a Phi Beta Kappa graduate in Physics from the University of Oklahoma, who co-founded the National Geophysical Company that was involved in oil and gas exploration. The house is one of the largest of Wright's career with over 10,000 square feet of living space. The family room is larger than that of the Coonley House (see UGL volume) at 23 by 34 feet and is surpassed by the 27 by 41 living room. The site is 7 acres with a creek on the eastern border. The undressed Texas sandstone is contrasted with a copper roof that extends into trellises. Gillin had three children; there are four family bedrooms and two servants' rooms. The house lacks the intimate residential appeal of Wright's Usonian Houses. Another Gillin project was a design for 'Aladdin,' in Hollywood (Opus #5528). c94

KALITA HUMPHREYS THEATER
(Dallas Theater Center)
3636 Turtle Creek Boulevard
Dallas, Texas 75219
1955 5514

GPS: N 32 48.658
W 96 48.067

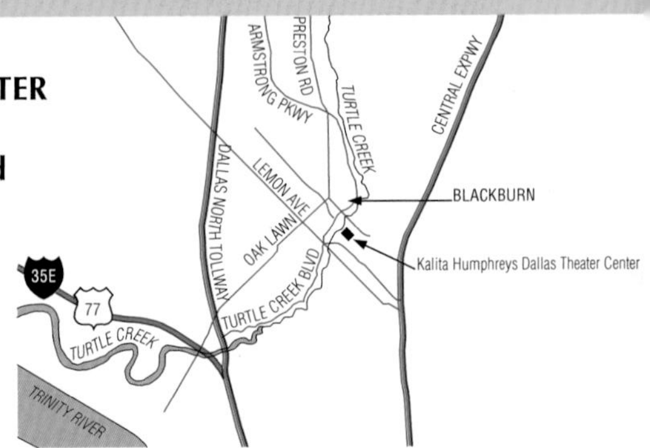

Directions: The theater is in the gully that runs parallel to Turtle Creek Boulevard. There are signs that direct the driver to its location between Blackburn and Lemon Avenue. It is about 2 miles northeast of the center of Dallas. To reach it take the Dallas North Tollway to Oak Lawn, from where it is signed.

Accessibility: The theater has regular performances.

■ The theater design has its roots in the 1916 project for Aline Barnsdall (p56). The plan is similar in many ways to the Community Christian Church, Kansas City (p118). Kalita Humphreys and her husband, Joe Burson, were both actors who died in a 1954 Pennsylvania plane crash. In 1959, Kalita's mother gave the theater group, which began in 1955, $100,000 as a memorial to them. John Rosenfield, a friend of Wright's, was responsible for putting his name forward as architect. Sylvan T Baer donated the site. Paul Baker, the managing director, was the primary contact, and he developed all the details of the scheme with Wright. The theater, which has only twelve wide rows, opened in 1959. One of the members of the executive committee was a Wright client Stanley Marcus (p99). c94

DALLAS SITES

See map on p96 for locations.

ROGERS LACY HOTEL SITE, Commerce, Evray and Jackson, Dallas 1946 4606

■ Wright's great champion, John Rosenfield of the *Dallas Morning News* (see also p98), was responsible for introducing him to Rogers E Lacy who commissioned the hotel. Lacy's parents died soon after he was born in 1884. Having left school in 5th grade, Lacy tried many types of work. He had several failed businesses before entering the oil business in 1931. By the time of his death he had acquired 134 oil wells and had become a well-known philanthropist. He was able to secure $26,000,000 in loans from two banks to build the hotel on a site in downtown Dallas. Unfortunately, however, he died just before construction was to begin.

The first nine floors of the hotel were to fill an entire city block and the next fifty-five floors were to form a tower. The hotel had one innovation that has become commonplace today, the interior skylit atrium. One of the most prominent examples of this is the Hyatt Peachtree Hotel in Atlanta designed by architect/developer John Portman. A second example is the Hyatt at the Embarcado Center, located just a few blocks north of the Morris Gift Shop in San Francisco (p28).

STANLEY MARCUS HOUSE SITE, Dallas, Texas 1935 3501

■ The site for this early Usonian design was a 6.5-acre parcel of land across from his father's property in Dallas. Before appointing Wright, Marcus interviewed several other architects, including the Modernist William Lescaze and the young Richard Neurtra. He was, however, unhappy with Wright's design, and assumed that Wright would not alter the plans to fit the $25,000 budget. Born in 1905, Harold Stanley Marcus, he was a graduate of 1925 and 1926 Harvard MBA, and began as the floor man at Neiman-Marcus store founded in 1907 by his uncle and his father. In November 1932, Marcus married fellow employee Mary Catrell.

HAROLD MARCUS HOUSING SITE, northeast of the intersection at Llano Road and Price Road, Dallas 1935 3505

This scheme was for a hundred houses on a site of 83 acres, north of Country Estates and Old Centerville Road, owned by Theo Marcus. The project did not develop very far. Only a few sketches remain.

WILLIAM L THAXTON HOUSE
12024 Tall Oaks, Bunker Hill
Houston, Texas 77024
1954 5414

GPS: N 29 46.000
W 95 32.369

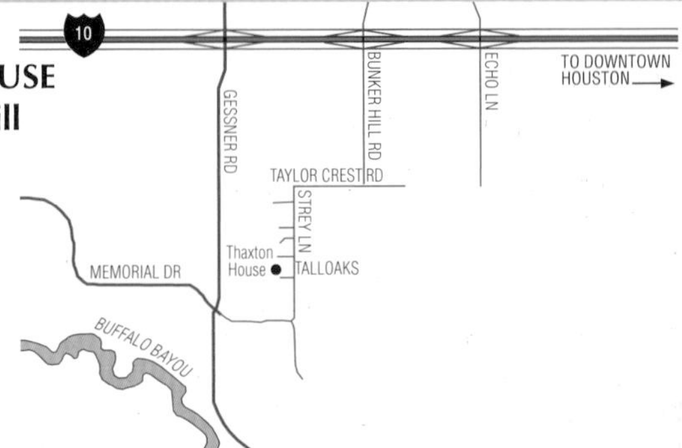

Directions: The house is west of downtown Houston, 5.5 miles west of Interstate 610 and south of Interstate 10. Exit I-10 at Bunker Hill Road and drive south 0.75 miles to Taylor Crest Road. Once on Taylor Crest keep going west 0.4 miles to Strey Lane. Drive south for 0.4 miles to Tall Oaks. The house is at the west end of Tall Oaks.

Accessibility: The house can be seen from the street through the gate.

■ William Thaxton was a retired insurance executive, who originally planned to build a housing development with John 'Davie' Davidson, near Memorial Drive. The 1.5-acre property at Tall Oaks cost about $5,200 and the house was originally budgeted at a modest $25-35,000, but totaled $125,000 by the time it was finished. Originally, it was 1,800 square feet with three bedrooms and a dark room. It was unusual for a house this far south to have an underfloor heating system. The house has had a difficult time with four additions, not all in keeping with the original concept. The house has, however, recently been purchased and a restoration program is underway. c98

TEXAS SITES

SAN ANTONIO TRANSIT ADMINISTRATION BUILDING SITE, San Pedro Park, San Antonio, Texas
1946 4725

■ D Gordon Rupe Jr and Laurence Wingerter were the principal speculators behind this building. It was proposed for a site between a ball park and San Pedro Park. The scheme included offices, an assembly hall and a bus terminal. In November 1946, the government restrictions on office building construction indefinitely postponed the project. Only a single rough sketch was executed.

SCHOOLHOUSE SITE, Crosbyton, Texas
1910 1008

■ This project was drawn up for Avery Coonley, for whom Wright had built a house in 1908 at Riverside, Illinois (see MetroChicago volume) and his three brothers. They owned the CB Livestock Company, a 79,000-acre cattle ranch at Crosbyton. They were responsible for founding the town when they moved the buildings and residents of nearby Emma in a land swap; they received one and a half acres for each acre of their land. The city has no evidence of a school built to Wright's design, but there exists a published perspective drawing of a town plan by William Drummond, who was employed in Wright's Oak Park Studio. Though the drawing is undated, Drummond worked with Coonley on his Riverside house in about 1910. The Coonley family was highly regarded by the townsfolk. His daughter, Elizabeth Ferry Coonley Faulkner, was invited to attend a reception in 1976 as an honorary guest. She recalled having briefly visited the town in 1917 on returning from a trip to Estes Park, Colorado (the site of the Horseshoe Inn, p87). The cattle venture nearly failed when there was a norther storm that killed over 3,000 cattle. It was saved, however, by the sale of a 40-mile railroad spur to the Santa Fe Railroad, which bisected the ranch and connected Crosbyton west to Lubbock.

ROBERT F WINDFOHR HOUSE SITE, Fort Worth, Texas
1949 4919

■ The design was for a large house with a circular living room. Its basic elements were included in at least two other proposals to clients but never built.

Robert Frairy Windfohr was born in Quantico, Maryland, in 1894. He graduated from Boston College. Having served as an artillery officer in World War I in Still, Oklahoma, he decided to stay in the West. His first 4,300-foot-deep oil well was dry but others, including several 1,000-barrel-a-day units were successful. He was involved in the Fort Worth Art Museum and several other civic organizations. In 1942, he married Anne Valiant Hall. The house was proposed for a site on the west side of town in the Westover Hills. He died in 1964 after a long illness. There is no apparent reason for his reluctance to build the Wright design. The Windfohr family remains a leading family in the Fort Worth area.

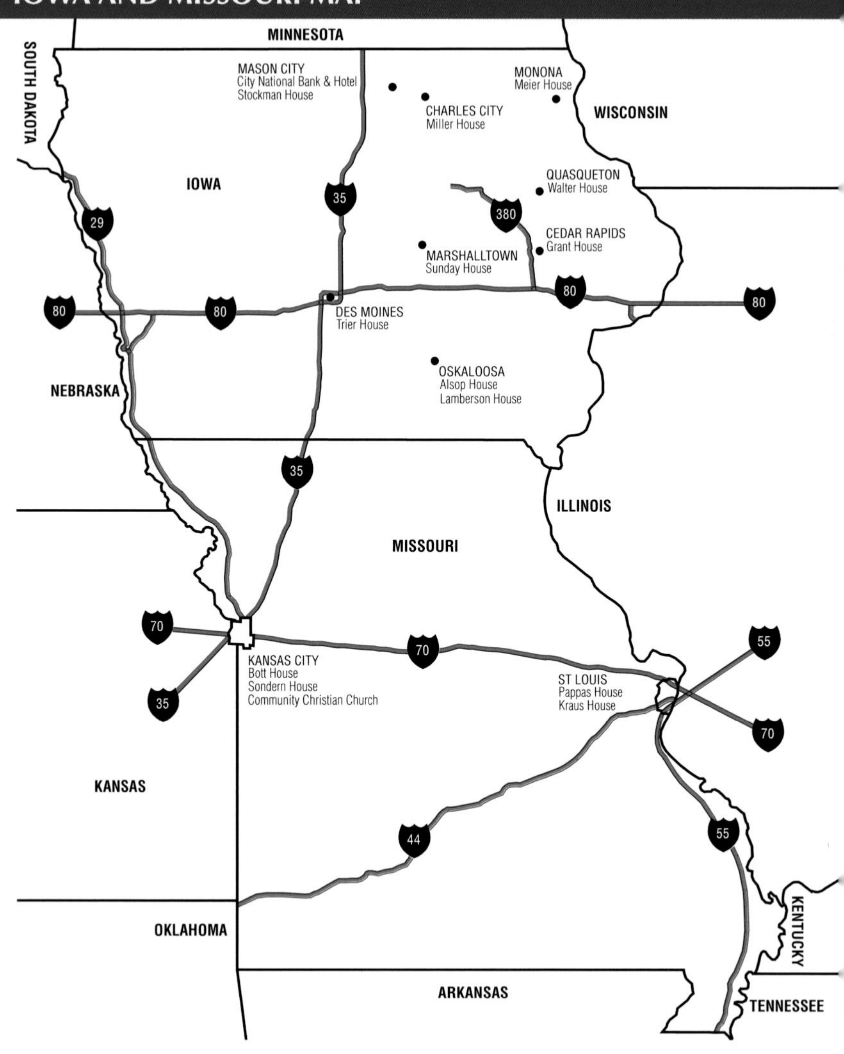

■ Most of the Wright buldings in Iowa and Missouri, with the exception of Mason City and Monona, were built between the mid forties and late fifties by clients of modest means. Rather than being referred or enticed to use Wright by family or associates, they heard about his work through magazines or the national press. In terms of climatic considerations and use of materials, the houses have a stronger affinity with Wright's other Midwestern works (see MetroChicago and UGL volumes), than those of the Far West. Wright was back on his home ground here. He spent his earliest childhood in Iowa. From 1869 to 1871 his father, William Carey Wright, was the preacher at McGregor

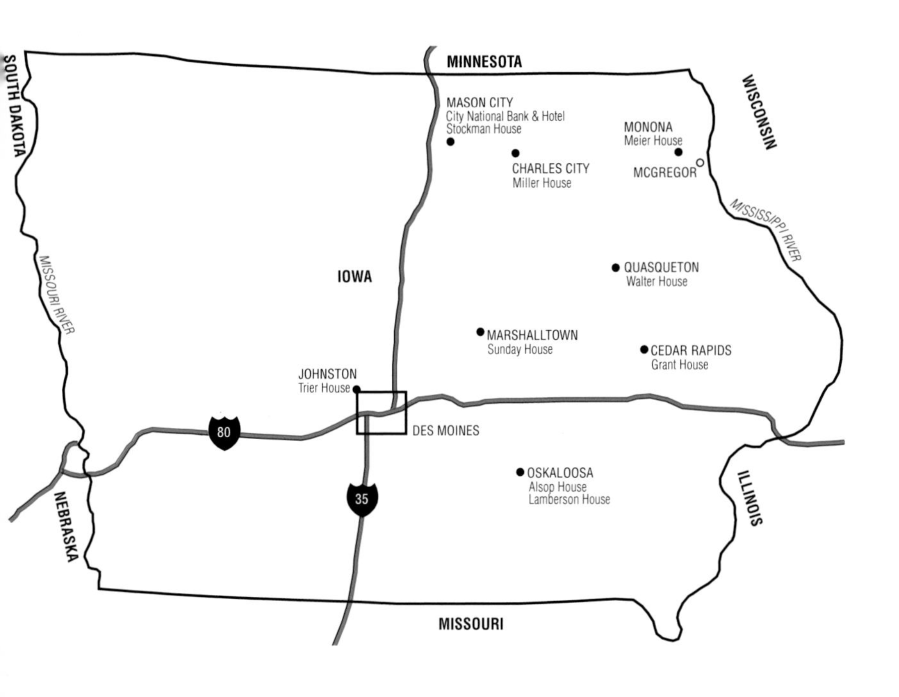

■ Iowa has a surprising number of Wright buildings. The first two commissions came about through JEE Markley, a parent of a child enrolled at Wright's aunts' Hillside Home School, for which Wright designed the premises (see UGL volume). The components for the American Systems House in Monona (p107) may have been transported by boat from Taliesin East down the Wisconsin River. One of the main group of houses designed during Wright's late career, the Alsop House (p113), was published in an important article that illustrated Wright's money-saving construction technique. Des Moines, along with Minneapolis and Chicago, possesses some of Wright's finest work.

CITY NATIONAL BANK AND HOTEL
5 West State Street
Mason City, Iowa 50401
1909 0902

GPS: N 43 09.103
W 93 12.109

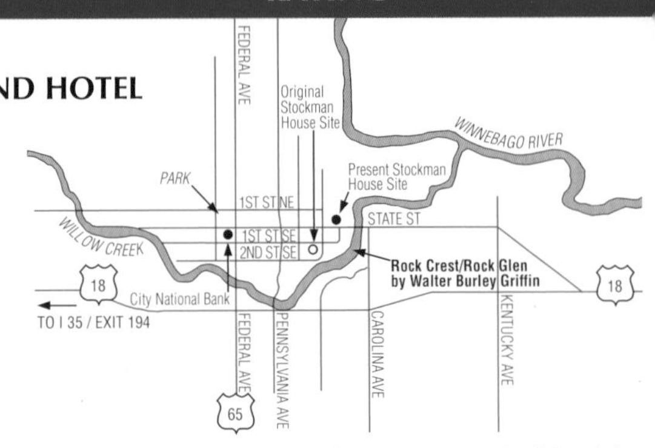

Directions: The building is located in the center of Mason City on the south side of the park. Exit Interstate 35 at Highway 18 and drive east for 0.1 miles to Federal Avenue and turn north for four blocks to State Street. The building is one block west on State Street.

Accessibility: The building can be seen from the street.

■ The buildings were originally designed to accommodate a bank at street level with offices above and a hotel to the west. Though the scale was devised to be in keeping with surrounding stores and offices, the hipped roof gives them a more residential feel.

The bank and hotel were commissioned by Blythe and JEE Markley, who first came into contact with Wright through Hillside School (see p102). These two prominent lawyers, were also behind the Rock Crest/Rock Glen Development of 1912 at Mason City designed by Wright's former assistant, Walter Burley Griffin. Wright drew up the Melson House of 1908 for a site on the bluff at Rock Crest. Though it was never realized, the design was developed, into a house for Isabel Roberts, an employee of Wright's, at River Forest (see MetroChicago volume). The bank and hotel were completed in September 1910. c72

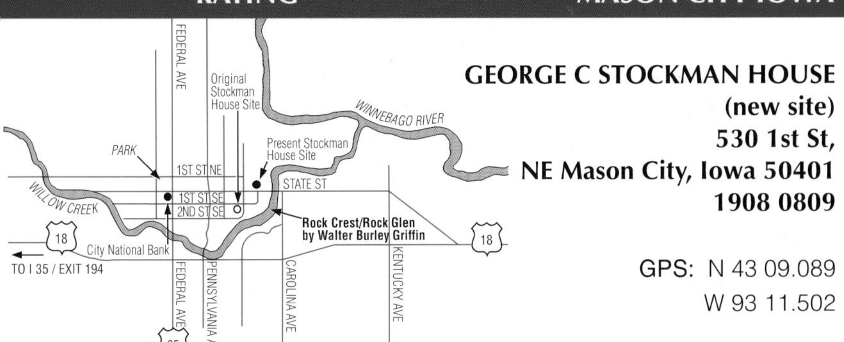

GEORGE C STOCKMAN HOUSE (new site)

530 1st St, NE Mason City, Iowa 50401

1908 0809

GPS: N 43 09.089
W 93 11.502

Directions: The house is five blocks east of the City National Bank and Hotel (see directions on p104), just north of State Street and west of Willow Creek.

Accessibility: The house can be seen from the street and there are tours of the interiors.

■ The house is a development of the April 1907 *Ladies Home Journal* Fireproof House for $5,000. It originally faced north and was on a site costing $2,250 at 311 SE 1st Street. In 1989, the house was moved to its present location.

George Stockman (1852-1927) was born in Mockwanago, Wisconsin. In 1888, he moved to Mason City, after training as a physician in Europe. It is most probable that Stockman and Wright met on one of Wright's trips to Mason City for the bank and hotel project, as Stockman was a friend of Markley. Stockman's wife, Eleanor, was involved in the women's suffrage movement. Stockman sold the house in 1918 for $11,000.

A visit to the Stockman House is a good opportunity to view the Rock Crest Development by Walter Burley Griffin (see also p104). There are ten outstanding examples of Prairie Houses on both sides of Willow Creek. c72

ALVIN MILLER HOUSE
1107 Court Street
Charles City, Iowa 50616
1946 5016

GPS: N 43 04.052
W 92 41.099

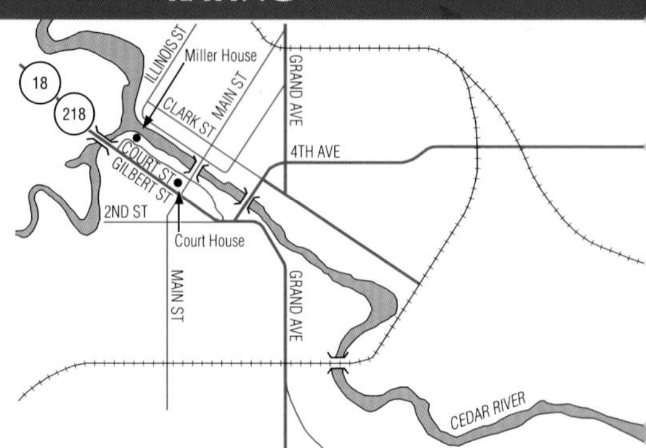

Directions: Take Main Street southwest from downtown Charles City over the river to the first street, which is Court Street. Turn north and drive to the end of the street. The house is on the east side of the street.

Accessibility: The house is visible from the street. It is easier to see the house from the park across the river.

■ Alvin Miller was born in 1880. He was sixty-six when he commissioned Wright to design his home and dental office. He lived in the house only twelve years before he died in 1963 at the age of seventy-three. He lived and went to school in Iowa and he was very active in the Boy Scouts. He was awarded the Silver Beaver, one of the highest civilian Boy Scouting awards. At $35,000, the house was a moderately expensive building. It was constructed by Moltz Construction company. The cabinets were made by the client's son. c74

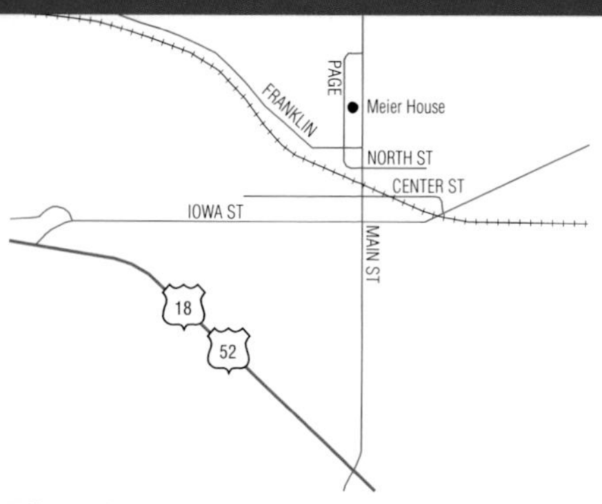

DELBERT W MEIER HOUSE
402 North Page
Monona, Iowa 52159
1917 1506

GPS: N 43 03.416
W 91 23.458

Directions: Exit Highway 18 at Main Street and drive north 2 miles to Franklin and then west one block to Page. Drive north to the address. The house is on the east side of the street.

Accessibility: The house can be seen from the street.

■ Born in 1880 on a farm near Pottsville, Delbert Meier attended Upper Iowa University in Fayette, before entering the University of Chicago in 1903. He received a Bachelor of Philosophy and a Law degree and graduated in 1906. He married Grace Burgess in December 1903, while he was still attending the University of Chicago. After living in Tulsa, Oklahoma, the Meiers moved to Monona, in 1908, to take over the law practice of Ed Otis. Meier wrote for the drawings, and had the building constructed by a local contractor without contacting Wright. c96

LOWELL WALTER HOUSE AND RIVER PAVILION

Cedar Rock Park
Quasqueton, Iowa 52326
1945 4505 (River Pavilion 1948 4813)

GPS: N 42 24.365
W 91 46.188

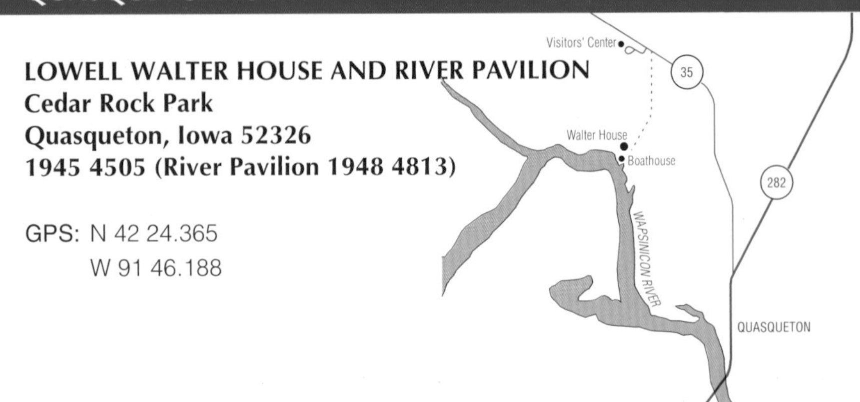

Directions: Exit Route 20 at Route 282 and go south for 4.5 miles on 282 to the intersection of Route W35. Turn to the Northwest on W35 and drive for a mile to the entrance where tours begin. The entrance is on the south side of the street.

Accessibility: The house is open regularly for tours from May through to October. Contact the Iowa Department of Natural Resources for details.

■ Planning for the Walter House started in 1945, construction began in 1948 and it was completed in 1950. Lowell Walter had been in contact with Wright since 1942 when he paved one of the roads below Taliesin. Not knowing who Wright was he asked him who owned Taliesin. Walter, who had invented an asphalt topping for country roads, did contracting work throughout Illinois, Wisconsin and Minnesota, as well as Iowa. He was born in Quasqueton in 1896 and moved to Des Moines, where he married Agnes Nielsen and founded the Iowa Road Builders Company. The Walters, who were childless, lived

in a two-bedroom bungalow. When Lowell Walter sold the Minnesota road operation in 1939 and the remains of his business in 1944, he started buying farms in the area. By 1943, he had acquired seventeen farms and 3,500 acres. In 1972, when he sold Arnold Farms, he had 5,000 acres. The site of the house, originally 11 acres, is now 400 acres and covers both sides of the Wapsipinicon River that passes the boathouse. Wright designed the house, the boathouse and the furniture, and was asked for his assistance in the choice of carpeting, drapes and even the housewares, plates, glassware and silverware. All of these remain with the house. The cost of the house is estimated to have been between $100,000 and $135,000.

The plaster soffits were beige, but were altered to brick red at Wright's suggestion. Both the roof and the floor are concrete. Unlike most other slab houses, the Walter House has removable concrete-floor panels that allow access to the underfloor heating system. The house was primarily a summer house for the Walters. The living room is 32 feet square.

The River Pavilion is anchored to an enormous boulder and contains space for his beautiful wooden boat and a guest room with a Pullman kitchen. It is a two-story design, which includes a large deck that overlooks the river.

Above the house is a large yard that contains a council ring similar to those designed by Jens Jensen, the landscape designer, who often worked with Wright.

The Walters left the house and grounds, along with a considerable trust fund for the maintenance of the property. This fund also provides for a stipend to the tour guides. His wood boat is on display at the visitor's center. All of the correspondence is now at the Iowa Historical Society in Des Moines. c96

DOUGLAS GRANT HOUSE
3400 Adel Drive SE
Cedar Rapids, Iowa 62403
1946 4503

GPS: N 42 00.654
W 91 37.359

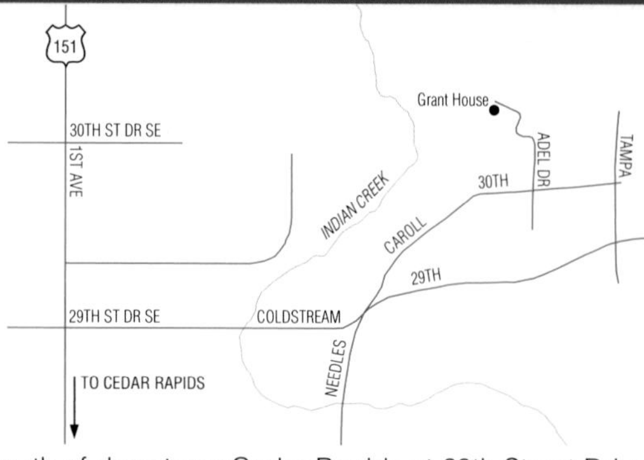

Directions: Exit Interstate 380 north of downtown Cedar Rapids at 29th Street Drive Southeast. Continue on 29th, which turns into Coldstream, carry on eastbound for 2 miles to Needles and turn northeast. Drive for one block onto Carroll and turn east onto 30th. Adel Drive is one block further east. Turn north and drive to the end of the street.

Accessibility: The house cannot be seen from the street.

■ The Grants were attracted to Wright's work in the 1938 January issue of *Architectural Forum.* They first contacted him in December 1945, and he invited them to Taliesin in the following May. They received the initial drawings in November 1946. Construction began in the summer of 1949 and they moved into the unfinished house in December 1950.

The entry is at the carport end of the house. It connects the living room, 127 feet away, with a hall with several sets of stairs. The site drops away at the entry level so that the living room is situated below the bedrooms. The Grants took two years to quarry the limestone and kept five masons busy on the stonework for a further two years. It took ten years to complete the house. Grant was in broadcasting – radio and then television. c76

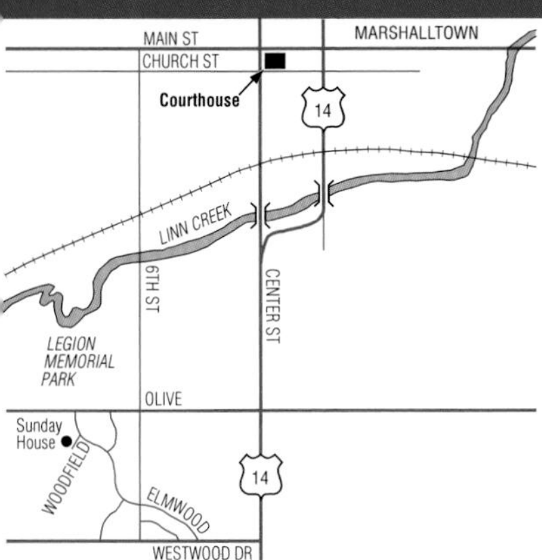

ROBERT H SUNDAY HOUSE
1701 Woodfield Drive
Marshalltown, Iowa 50158
1955 5522

GPS: N 42 01.583
W 92 55.651

Directions: The house is southwest of downtown Marshalltown and 1.2 miles north of Interstate 30. It is half a mile west of Iowa Route 14 between Olive and Westwood, west of South 6th Street. Turn south onto Woodfield to the end of the street, one block.

Accessibility: The house can not be seen from the street.

■ Robert Sunday grew up in Marshalltown, where his father owned the local lumber company. He trained as an architect in the Masters program at Iowa State University, and later set up a construction business. While in the Navy, he was stationed just north of Chicago and visited many of Wright's Midwest buildings.

The house is similar in plan to the Usonian Exhibition House that was on the site of the Guggenheim Museum in New York (Opus #4305). Sunday initially wanted to have the house designed solely in one material, using Wright's Usonian Automatic block system. However, he asked to have the house redesigned using brick and wood. c96

PAUL J TRIER HOUSE
6880 NW Beaver Drive
Johnston (Des Moines), Iowa 50131
1957 5724

GPS: N 41 41.163
W 93 41.368

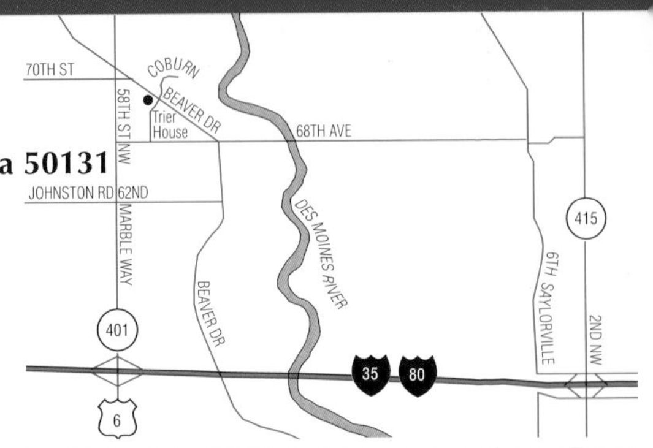

Directions: Johnston is just north of Interstate 35/80. Exit Interstate 35/80 at Route 401, Marble Way, which turns into 58th Street, and drive north for 2.6 miles to Beaver Drive and turn to the southeast for 0.6 miles. The house is on the east side of the street.

Accessibility: The house can be seen from the street.

■ The ceilings of this house vary from 6 feet 8 inches in the bedrooms to 10 feet 9 inches in the living room. Like the Feiman House of Canton, Ohio (Opus #5408), the Trier House is based on the Usonian Exhibition House that was built on the site of the Guggenheim Museum in New York (see also p111). The house was fully furnished with Wright-designed furniture that was built by the Triers. c96

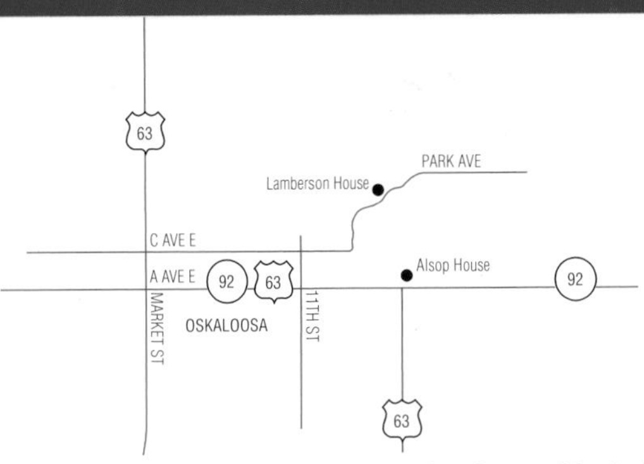

CAROLL ALSOP HOUSE
1907 A Avenue East
Oskaloosa, Iowa 52577
1948 4804

GPS: N 41 17.806
W 92 37.831

Directions: From Highway 63 take Route 92, A Avenue East, eastwards, through downtown Oskaloosa. Take it for 0.7 miles to the house on the north side of the street.

Accessibility: The house can be seen from the street.

■ Like Jack Lamberson (p114), who built the other Wright house in Oskaloosa, Caroll Alsop was a World War II veteran – both houses were designed immediately after the war in 1948. Alsop owned a women's ready-to-wear department store in the town. He did not retire until the early 1970s when he moved to Minnesota.

A wonderful article was published in the March 1962 issue of *House & Home,* describing the house's construction. A considerable amount of furniture was designed by Wright for the living and dining rooms. The roll of the hill and the placement of the house near a small lake, with its views to east and the south, gives it probably one of the most beautiful sites of all of Wright's buildings. c72

JACK LAMBERSON HOUSE
511 North Park Avenue
Oskaloosa, Iowa 52577
1948 4712

GPS: N 41 18.151
W 92 37.451

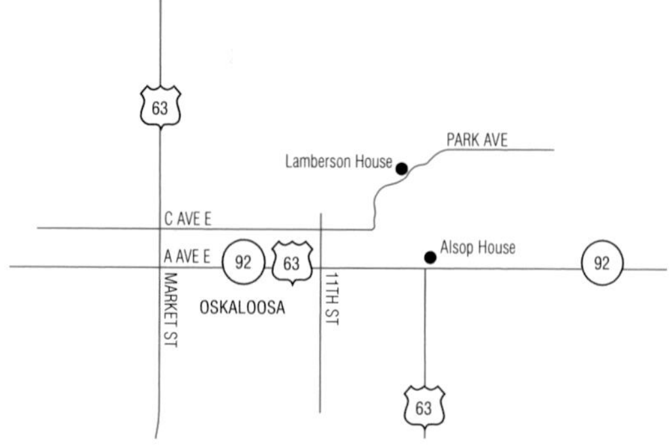

Directions: As with the Alsop House, the Lamberson House is east and north of downtown Oskaloosa. From Highway 63, take A Avenue East to 11th Street to the north, which is just before the Alsop House. Turn off at C Avenue East to the east and drive for 0.2 miles till it changes into Park Avenue, and continue for half a mile to the house on the west side of the street.

Accessibility: The house can be seen from the street.

■ This was the first of the two Oskaloosa houses. Alice Lamberson introduced the idea of using Wright to both the Alsops (p113) and her husband 'Jack', John L Lamberson. Jack was the Secretary Treasurer of the family's Ford-Mercury and Ford tractor dealership. By 1951, the Lambersons had moved out of the house and Jack was listed as a farmer in the city directory.

The house is unique for its triangular grid and hipped roof. The kitchen is lit from above by a skylight rather than a window. The dining-room chairs were designed by Wright. c73

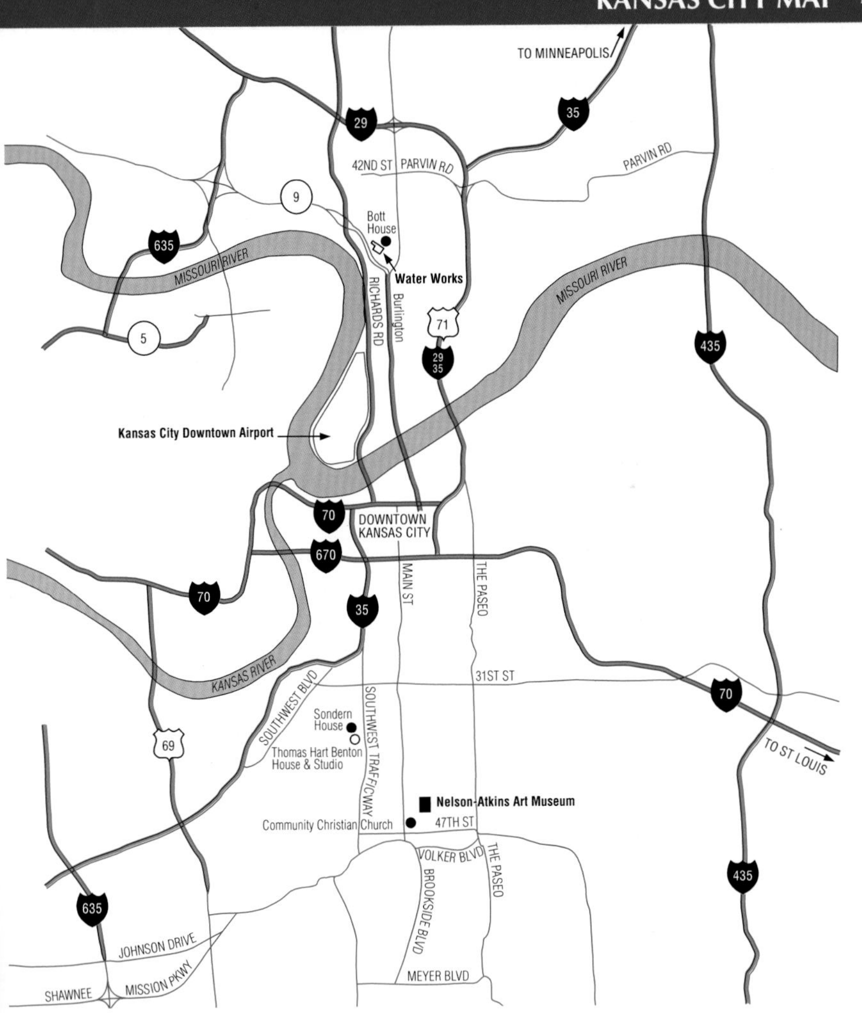

■ It was surprising to find that the Sondern House (p117) is next door to the house and studio of one of North America's most important artists, Thomas Hart Benton. This State Historic Site appears on many Kansas City and Missouri State maps. Benton lived here from 1939 until his death in 1975. From his house, he must have had a wonderful view of the initial construction of the Sondern House, as well as the additions made to it by its second owners, the Adlers. There is also a first rate art museum, the Nelson-Atkins Art Galleries, a few blocks east of the Community Christian Church (p118). The Bott House (p116) is the most difficult to locate and there is little to see of the exterior, unless one is fortunate enough to be invited in to see the interior.

FRANK BOTT HOUSE
3640 NW Briarcliff Road
Kansas City, Missouri 64116
1956 5627

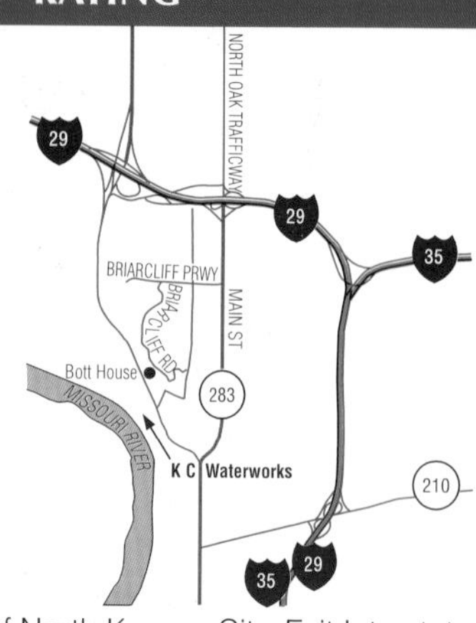

GPS: N 39 09.610
W 94 3.112

Directions: The house is north of the airport and of North Kansas City. Exit Interstate 29 at Main Street, west of Interstate 35 and drive south onto North Oak Trafficway, Route 283, for 0.6 miles to Briarcliff Parkway at the traffic light and turn west for 0.5 miles to the stop sign at Briarcliff Road. Turn south for 0.8 miles to the address.

Accessibility: Only a small portion of the top floor can be seen across the concrete court. The house can be seen from Highway 9 above the waterworks.

■ Eloise Bott always dreamed of having a house on a hill overlooking water. She first came across Wright when she saw his picture on the cover of the 17 January 1938 issue of *Time* magazine

Construction started on the Bott House in 1961, it was built with stone from the farm. The four-story volume is cantilevered from a central spine in a similar way to that of the Price Tower (p92). Eloise Bott lived in the four-bedroom house until her death in 1987. c96

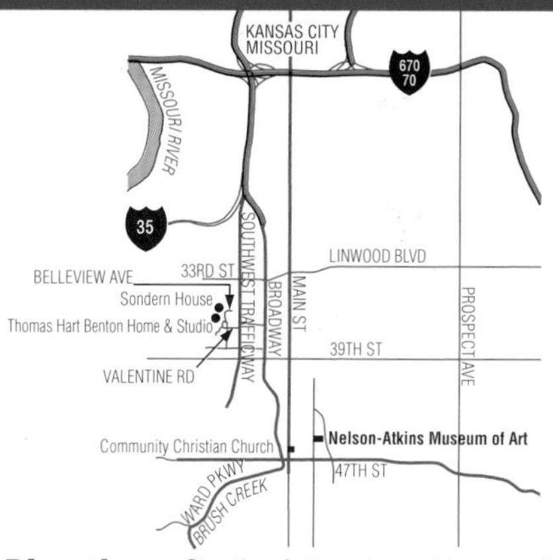

CLARENCE SONDERN HOUSE

3600 Belleview Avenue
Kansas City, Missouri 64111
1940 4014

GPS: N 39 03.908
W 94 30.136

Directions: South of downtown Kansas City and Interstate 70, take the Interstate 35 extension, the Southwest Trafficway, about 1.5 miles to the traffic light at Valentine Road and turn west for 2 blocks to Belleview Avenue and go north half a block. The house is on the west side of the street to the north of the Thomas Hart Benton House.

Accessibility: A small part of the roof of the house can be seen from the street down a long drive. Proceeding down the drive, however, would impinge on the privacy of the residents.

■ The 1,000-square-foot house was originally commissioned in 1940 by a chemist, Clarence Sondern, who sold it in 1942 to Virginia Oppenheimer. After Oppenheimer married Arnold Adler, the Adlers asked Wright for a 2,000-square-foot addition (Opus #4907), as well as a swimming pool and fish pond. The house was sold again in 1964. The current residents are intending to give it to the nearby Nelson Art Gallery. c96

COMMUNITY CHRISTIAN CHURCH
4601 Main Street
Kansas City, Missouri 64112
1940 4004

GPS: N 39 02.607
W 94 35.184

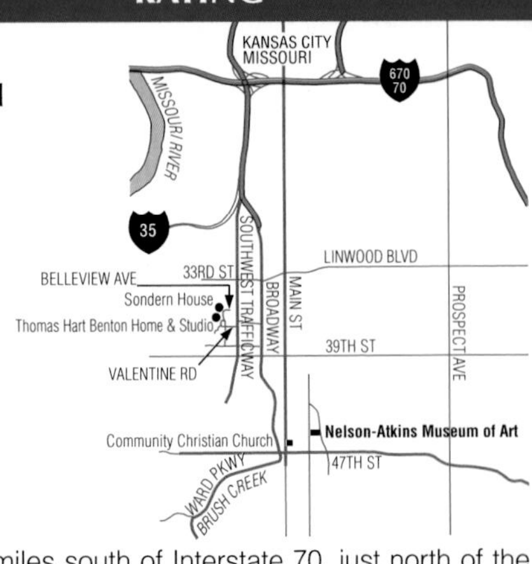

Directions: The church is in the city 3.5 miles south of Interstate 70, just north of the corner of 47th Street on Main Street, about half a mile east of the Southwest Trafficway.

Accessibility: The church can be seen from the street.

■ This church was built for the First Christian Church (founded 1888) to replace an earlier structure that burned down on Halloween night, 1939. Wright was approached to design a fireproof church because of the success of his earthquake-proof design for the Imperial Hotel, Tokyo (pp129-31). There was a budget of $175,000. The construction supervisor was Vic Holm of Ben E Wiltcheck, who had worked on Wright's buildings in Racine. The foundations were a point of contention between Wright and the city's building inspectors; Wright favored crushed stone, or ballast, rather than traditional poured concrete footing. The new church was dedicated on 4 January 1942. The lights emanating from the roof, pointing heavenward, have operated at weekends since 1994. c96

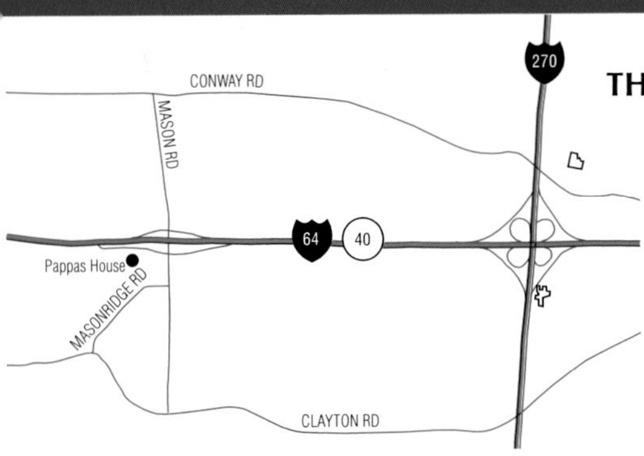

THEODORE A PAPPAS HOUSE
8654 Masonridge Road
St Louis, Missouri 63141
1955 5516

GPS: N 38 38.202
W 90 29.036

Directions: Exit Interstate 64 at Mason Road and drive south one block to Masonridge Road. Turn west for about 200 feet to the house which is on the north side.

Accessibility: The house can not be seen from the street.

■ While the Pappases were living in Milwaukee, Bette persuaded her husband to take a tour of the Johnson Wax Company in Racine (see UGL volume). They became hooked on Wright. In 1947, they moved to St Louis, where Ted worked for the Public Relations Department of St Louis Browns (later Cleveland Browns), and they bought 8 acres. On 28 July 1954, they wrote to Wright requesting that he design them a single-story house – they cleverly enclosed a $300 retainer. After they received preliminary drawings in October 1955, Wright invited them to Taliesin West to approve the final plans. When they had twins on 15 September 1956, they wrote to Wright asking for another bedroom. In November 1959, they sold the original 8-acre plot and found a lot closer to downtown. After going through four contractors, and having their loan recalled through lack of progress, they moved in on 6 October 1964. c84

RUSSELL KRAUS HOUSE
120 North Ballas Road
Kirkwood, Missouri 63122
1951 5123

GPS: N 38 34.990
W 90 26.630

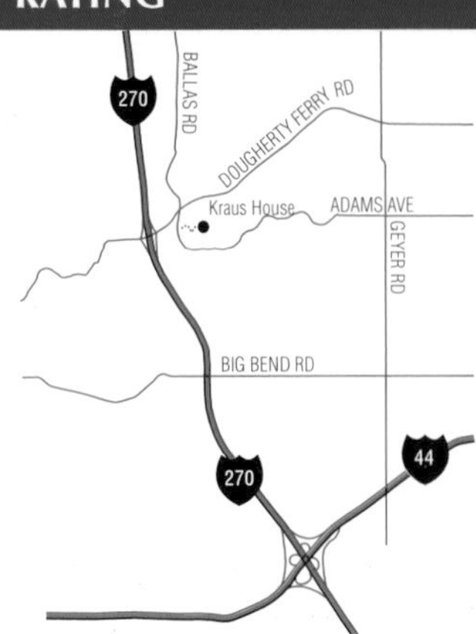

Directions: Kirkwood is on the southwest side of St Louis. Take Interstate 44 southwest to Interstate 270, and then drive north 2 miles to Dougherty Ferry Road. After 0.3 miles take an easterly turning off to Ballas Road. The entry to the 10-acre property is 0.1 miles south of Dougherty Ferry Road on the east side of Ballas.

Accessibility: The house is off the road up a private drive.

■ Russell Kraus was an advertising artist and writer for Coca-Cola and Anheiser Bush. His office was in Adler & Sullivan's Wainwright Building in St Louis. Wright came to the Krauses' attention when they read an article by Loren Pope in the August 1948 issue of *House Beautiful* magazine. Ruth was fourteen years older than Russell, and they first wrote to Wright in 1949, soon after they were married, when they decided to have a Wright-designed house rather than children. Over 150 pages of correspondence survive between Wright and Kraus. It took about four years for them to agree on the final plans. c96

HAWAII AND WESTERN CANADA SITES

See map pp14-15 for locations.

MARTIN PENCE HOUSE SITE, Hilo, Hawaii 4019 1940

■ Martin Pence was the County Attorney for Hawaii. After he saw the 1938 January issue of *Architectural Forum*, he wrote to Wright in January 1939 asking for a house costing between $5,000 and $6,000. By April 1939, Pence had sent a large package of information about the site and climate to Wright. In his reply, Wright mentioned that he often stopped in Hawaii en route to Japan and was somewhat familiar with it. By March 1949, Pence had set up on his own as an attorney and felt forced to tell Wright he would not be able to build in the immediate future. Wright was very gracious and invited Pence to visit in Arizona, and asked him to let him know if things changed.

BANFF NATIONAL PARK PAVILION SITE, Banff, Alberta, Canada 1911 1302

■ Francis C Sullivan, who probably worked as a draftsman in Wright's Oak Park Studio, in about 1907, brought Wright this Canadian project. It may have been an attempt to boost Wright's practice in 1911, after his return from his 1909 sojourn with Mamah Cheney. Sullivan himself was working in eastern Canada from his office in Ottawa, Ontario, on a design for the Carnegie Library in Pembroke, Ontario. Wright's pavilion was designed for Banff in western Canada, just west of Calgary, near Lake Louise, in the Rocky Mountains.

By August 1913, the pavilion was largely completed. The building was a one-story stone and horizontal board and batten structure that comprised a large central space with facilites for men and women. A small kitchen and caretaker's room filled the rest of the interior. Some of the stonework has been reported to be still extant in the park, if one looks hard enough. Its exact location is undocumented.

MEXICO AND CENTRAL AMERICA MAP

■ Wright and his wife Olgivanna visited Acapulco as guests of the Mexican cabinet minister Raul Bailleres to discuss designing a house for him and to see the intended site. Of all the Mexican projects, this design probably had the greatest chance of being completed. Unfortunately political events interceded. Unlike many of the US regions, the Mexican clients cannot be shown to have formed any kind of independent network. They do not appear to have been related through business or through family ties. It is unclear from the documents if Wright or any of his apprentices ever visited any of these Mexican or Central American sites or clients.

MEXICAN AND CENTRAL AMERICAN SITES

See map on p122 for locations.

RAUL BAILLERES HOUSE, Acapulco, Mexico
1952 5202

■ Raul Bailleres (see also p122) first heard about Wright when he was at the Mayo Clinic in Rochester, Minnesota, where there were a number Wright houses in the area. On 15 May 1952, he wrote to Wright asking him to design him a house. Upon Bailleres' invitation, Wright visited his cliff-side property, which was covered with large boulders. Wright discussed the possibility of making the house air conditioned throughout. In September 1952, Bailleres informed Wright of a problem with the land title that had to be corrected. In March 1953, he told Wright that the government was taking the land to enlarge the Federal Shipping yards. The project had to be abandoned. The design is an adaptation of the drawings for the Robert Windfohr House (p101).

HELEN SOTTIL HOUSE, Curnevaca, Mexico
1956 5722

■ This house was commissioned by Helen Sottil, who was acting on behalf of some people called Pope from Minneapolis about whom nothing is know. Sottil lived in San Antonio, Texas, and was married to Donald Wilkie, who had already employed Wright to design an unbuilt house for him in Hennepin County, Minnesota (Opus #4719). The Sottil House was to have three bedrooms and bathrooms, with accommodation for servants and a swimming pool. It was to have a total of about 5,000 square feet and cost about $20,000. The Sottils got a set of magnificent plans in December 1956. Though Helen Sottil wanted the design revised, this never happened and the house remained unbuilt.

JJ VALLARINO HOUSE, Panama City, Panama
1951 5113, 5118, 5127

■ Three variations of this project were produced during a four-year period. Nothing is known about the clients.

FREUND Y CIA DEPARTMENT STORE, San Salvador, El Salvador
1955 5425

■ This was to be a three-story department store building quite similar to the 1931 *Capitol Journal* Building, for Salem, Oregon (Opus #310). It adopts the same dendriform columns used in the Johnson Wax Company, Racine, Wisconsin (see UGL volume). Curiously, no correspondence survives for this late project.

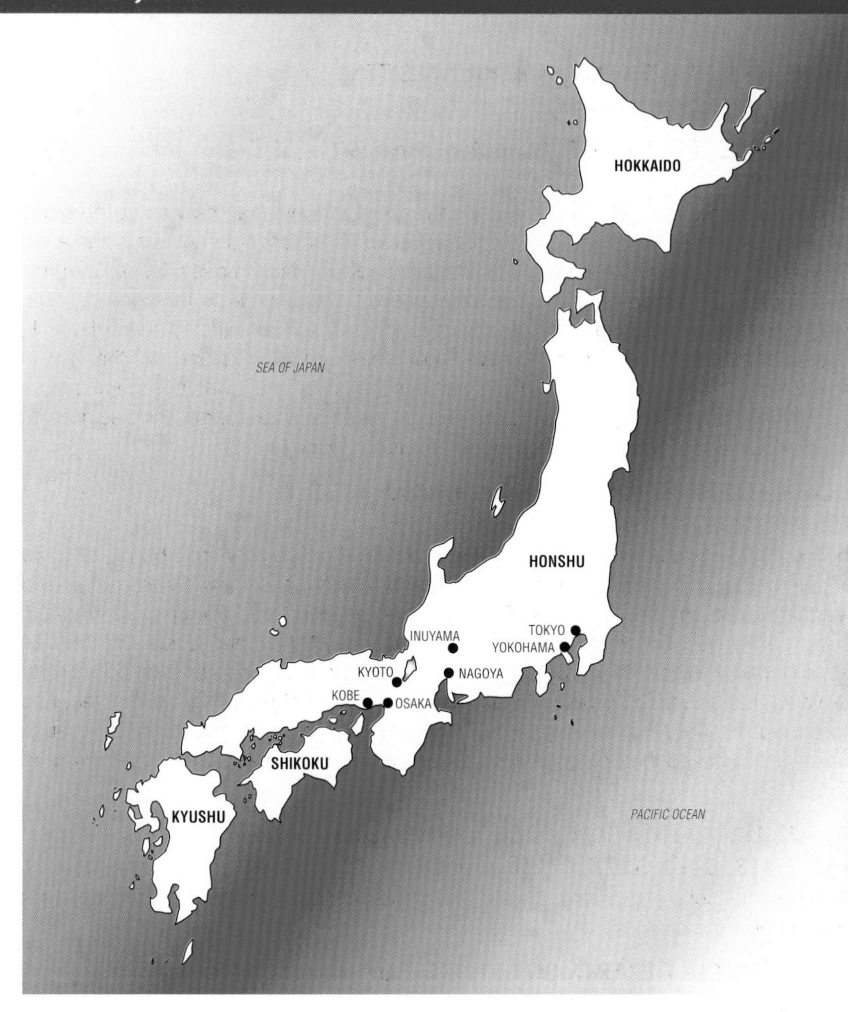

■ Wright referred to Japan as, 'the most romantic, artistic country on earth.' He was introduced to Japanese art and culture in 1880s Chicago through his first employer, Joseph Lyman Silsbee, who had his own collection of Japanese artifacts. Wright hosted parties where the guests came dressed in kimonos and his home was decorated with paper lanterns – though it is unlikely that the theme extended as far as the food.

Wright himself began collecting Japanese prints and quickly became a dealer, supplying prints to collections that included the Art Institute of Chicago and the Spaulding Collection in New England; he also often gave or sold them to his clients. He put on exhibitions of his print collection at the Chicago Art Institute in1906, 1908 and 1917.

The first exhibit was designed by Wright and included special print frames for some of the prints, designed by him and his son John.

Wright's initial trip to Japan was in 1905 and lasted ten weeks. He was accompanied by his first wife, Catherine Tobin Wright and his clients, Cecelia and Ward Willits of Highland Park (see MetroChicago volume). On this first visit, he went to most of the cities where he gained his Japanese commissions. Otherwise he traveled to Japan purely on business, mainly when he was designing and supervising the Imperial Hotel (pp129-31) as well as other Japanese commissions. It is curious that, despite his early passion for the country, Wright never returned to Japan after 1923.

■ Tokyo contains the greatest concentration of Wright's designs. While the Imperial Hotel (pp129-31) was a very popular attraction, before it was demolished in 1968, too few people were able to appreciate it. Though this building is well documented in black and white, there are few color shots of the interior. A reconstruction of part of the hotel, using much of the building's original fabric has taken some sting out of the loss (pp130-31). Nevertheless, moving it to a remote location has placed it in an alien and inappropriate context.

It can only be hoped that lessons learned in the Imperial Hotel will be absorbed in the conservation of Jiyu Gakuen School of the Free Spirit (p127). It is most essential that the scale of the school and its relationship with its surrounding neighborhood is maintained in order to experience it as Wright intended it.

It is also worth visiting the buildings of the Czech-American Antonin Raymond and the Japanese Arato Endo (see p127), who worked for Wright in Japan. Raymond was the supervising architect on the Imperial Hotel. He built his own house at Reinanzaka in 1923 and formed a practice in Tokyo with his wife Noemi Pernessin.

Tokyo is a wonderful city for pedestrians, and thus this section of the guide is designed for those traveling by foot and public transport rather than for drivers.

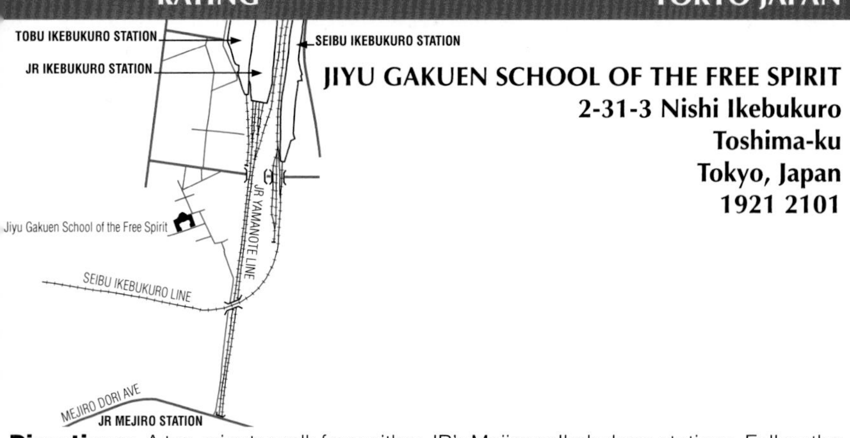

JIYU GAKUEN SCHOOL OF THE FREE SPIRIT

2-31-3 Nishi Ikebukuro
Toshima-ku
Tokyo, Japan
1921 2101

Directions: A ten-minute walk from either JR's Mejiro or Ikebukuro stations. Follow the signs to 'Fujin-no-tomo-sha.'

Accessibility: The school can be seen from the street.

■ Since the school moved out of the building to a Tokyo suburb, it has become a college for amateur craftsmen, and is referred to as 'Myonichikan.' A wood and plaster building, set at ground level, the school is deteriorating with the damp of the Japanese climate. The central and west wings are thought to have been completed before Wright left Japan, but the east wing was not finished until 1926 by Arato Endo.

AISAKU HAYASHI HOUSE
1-1-30, Komazawa
Setagaya-ku
Tokyo, Japan
1917 1702

Directions: A five-minute walk up the hill from the back exit of JR's Odawara Station.

Accessibility: The house cannot be seen from the road.

■ Aisaku Hayashi was the manager of the Imperial Hotel. The house was completed early during the period of Wright's work in Japan (he visited on business at least five times between 1918 and 1923) in gratitude for Hayashi getting him the commission for the hotel.The original roof, which is similar to those seen on Shinto shrines with singles and short cross beams arranged along the ridge, has recently been restored. Only the living room remains true to Wright's original design. The other rooms have been converted into tatami rooms. It is now owned by the advertising company Dentsu and used as a guest house, known as 'Hassei-en.' c86

IMPERIAL HOTEL SITE
(Original hotel demolished 1968)
1-1 Uchisaiwai-cho
Chiyoda-ku
Tokyo, Japan
1915 1509, 1409,
(Annex 1604)
(Powerhouse 1611)

Directions: A five-minute walk south from JR's Yuhraku-cho Station or just in front of the exit of the Metro's Hibiya Station of the Hibiya or Chiyida lines.

Accessibility: The new hotel building is open at all times.

■ This is the location of Wright's original Imperial Hotel. Situated across from the Imperial Palace, the 4-acre site of Wright's original hotel is probably one of the most valuable pieces of real estate in the world. For this reason, Wright's spread out low-rise structure was demolished in 1968 to make away for a more profitable use of the property and the construction of the high-rise hotel, which now takes its place. In the new hotel, the original mural and fireplace have been relocated in the bar. Occasionally, there are small Wright exhibits in the lobbies. c23

IMPERIAL HOTEL RECONSTRUCTION
Museum at Meiji-mura
1 Uchiyama
Inuyama City,
Aichi Prefecture
Nagoya, Japan
1976 1509

Directions: A twenty-minute bus ride from the Inuyama Station of the Meitetsu Inuyama line. The site of the old Imperial Hotel is shown on the signboard at the entrance.

Accessibility: The park is open all year and access to the reconstruction is unlimited while visiting the park.

■ The Imperial Hotel in Tokyo (p129) was reconstructed in the Museum Meiji-mura in 1976, after it was demolished in 1968. It was made possible by the railroad company, Nagoya Tetsudo, who own the museum, through the collaborative efforts of the President of the company, Moto-o Tsuchikawa and the architect Yoshiro Taniguchi. Kajima Construction Co, who demolished the hotel in Tokyo, also worked on its reconstruction.

Wright's Imperial Hotel was not the first of its kind in Tokyo. The first hotel for westerners was built in 1887 by the Imperial Household. When, however, the US annexed the Philippines in 1902 Japan became a stopover point. By 1910, the first package tour

arrived and plans were launched to build a new hotel. In 1912, a Chicago banker friend of Wright's, Frederick W Gookin, recommended him to the managing director of the Imperial, Aisaku Hayashi, for the job, and in early 1912 he traveled to Tokyo for preliminary meetings. Construction was, however, postponed by the death of Emperor Meiji in 1912 and World War I. The first phase of the hotel was not opened until July 1922.

From the beginning, Wright's Imperial Hotel was beset by catastrophe. On 16 April 1922, while the Prince of Wales was in residence, a fire broke out in the original hotel building, burning it to the ground. Fortunately, the fire occurred in the afternoon so there were no injuries or deaths; the Prince and his entourage were at the Imperial Palace attending a garden party. The remainder of the hotel was completed on 1 September 1923, the day before the Kanto earthquake, the worst ever experienced in Japan. The epicenter of the quake was 10 miles into the earth. It devastated Tokyo and Yokohama. Over 100,000 people died in Tokyo alone. The hotel, however, had suffered such minimal damage that it became an oasis for refugees; power and water was restored to it within four days. In ensuing months, it was transformed into a headquarters for embassies and relief organizations. Another quake, half the power of the Kanto, hit on 24 January 1924.

It was the Assistant Manager, Tetsuzo Inumaru, who sent Wright the telegram in 1923 to tell him that the Imperial had withstood the earthquake. Inumaru had worked in Europe's and New York's most prestigious hotels. His understanding of the West made Wright the proper choice for the hotel, which had to span Eastern and Western cultures.

After World War II, the hotel served as the headquarters for General MacArthur and the Army of Occupation. In March 1952, its management was returned to the owners.

The reconstruction of the hotel exemplifies a most successful earthquake-proof design and contributes to an understanding of Wright's use of space during the period in which it was built. c85

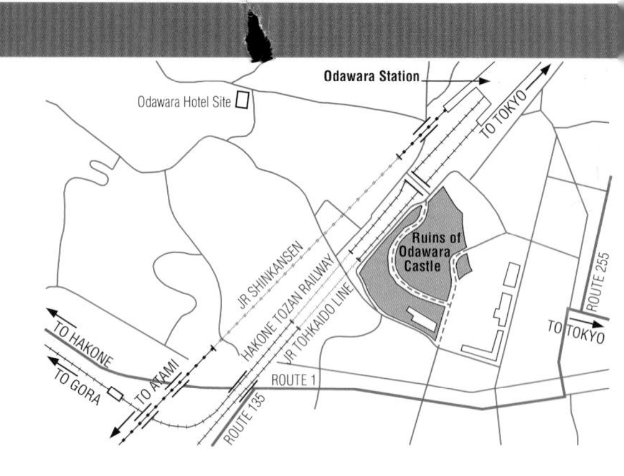

JAPANESE SITES

See maps on pp125 and 126 for locations, and above for Odawara Hotel Site and Fukuhara House Site.

AMERICAN EMBASSY SITE, Tokyo
1914 1406

■ This project is a mystery. There is no evidence that this building was ever commissioned. Wright may have produced it to demonstrate his ability to design a public building to the Imperial Hotel Board of Directors. It may be a modification of the Thaxter Shaw House for Montreal, Canada, with symmetrical wings (Opus #0610). The original drawing is in the Library of Congress in Washington.

VISCOUNT INOUE HOUSE SITE, Tokyo
1918 1804

■ This house design was one of six produced for Viscount Inoue. Professor Tanigawa came into contact with the widow of Viscount Tadashiro Inoue Kanako Inouse, who gave the six drawings to the College of Engineering at Nihon University, where they remain. The design was for a large two-story residence of reinforced concrete, brick and Oya stone similar to the Imperial Hotel. It included a three car garage with chauffeur's quarters. Drawings formerly attributed to another project, Immu (Opus #1802), are now thought to belong to this scheme.

ARINOBU FUKUHARA HOUSE SITE, 1300-4 Gohra, Hakone, Kanagawa Prefecture
1918 1801

■ This design was executed for the founder of the Shishedo Cosmetic Company. It was a second home in a resort area of Gohra. It was extant for only about three years before being destroyed in the Kanto earthquake of 1923. The drawings are dated 19 September 1919. A photo was published of it in 1924, as an example of great architecture that was lost. The house was a wooden structure in Wright's Prairie mode. Wright's mother, Anna, visited it on her trip to Japan in 1920.

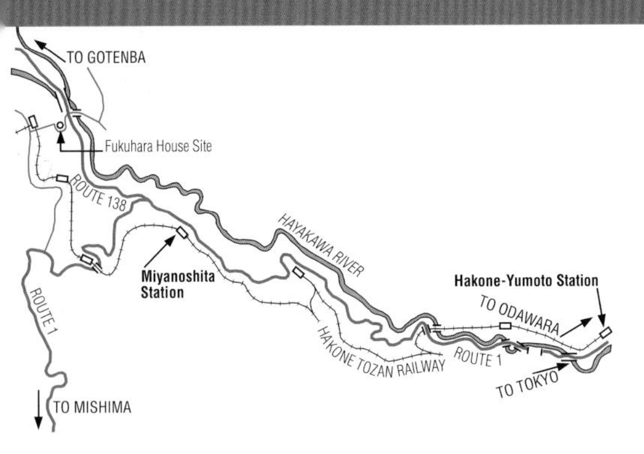

MIHARA HOUSE SITE, Tokyo
1918 1807

■ Next to nothing is known about the client or the site, and there are only two sheets of drawings. The design is similar in style to those for Los Angeles at about the same time. The house was small. It was confused in the past with the Freeman House (p54), as the Freeman drawings got mistakenly put in the Mihara House file in the archives of the Frank Lloyd Wright Foundation.

SITE OF MOTION PICTURE THEATER FOR GINZA, Tokyo
1918 1805

■ There are no existing drawings for this project, only a very detailed 1:50 plaster model that shows the interior arrangement of a central stage, thought to be for Sumo wrestling. Wright gave it to the School of Architecture at Kyoto University.

BARON GOTO HOUSE SITE, near Kamakura
(1917) 1921 2105

■ Only a few of Wright's sketches survive for this house. It is difficult to determine from them what the building would have looked like. It may have been intended as a guest house for the Mayor of Tokyo, Shinpei Goto. In 1922, Goto commissioned Antonin Raymond, Wright's former assistant at the Imperial Hotel, to design a guest house for the Goto estate.

ODAWARA HOTEL SITE,
3 Shiroyama, Odawara City, Kanagawa Prefecture
1917 1706

■ Only three drawings exist for this building. It was commissioned in 1917 by the Mayor Hironosuke Imai as a part of an amusement park. The hotel was to have been a resort rather than an urban hotel like the Imperial. Although no photographs of the hotel are known of, it was noted on a tourist map of 1932.

TAZAEMON YAMAMURA HOUSE
3-10 Yamate-cho
Ashiya City, Hyogo Prefecture
Japan
1918 1803

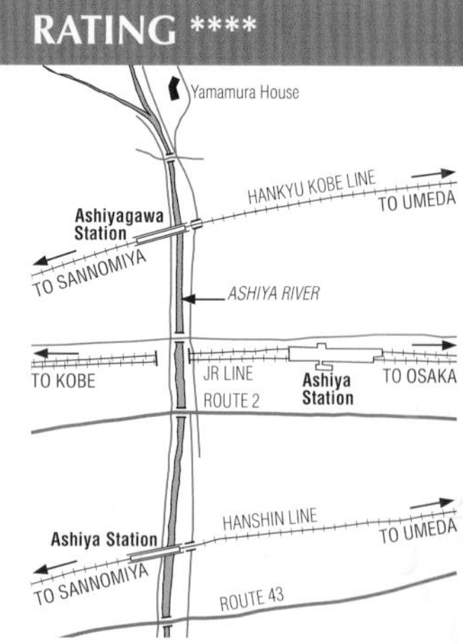

Directions: A five-minute walk to the north from Ashiyagawa Station on the Hankyu-Kobe line or a fifteen-minute walk north from JR's Ashiya Station.

Accessibility: The house is owned by the Yodogawa Steel Company and open several days a week.

■ Yamamura was a sake maker. Hoshijima and Arato Endo were high-school classmates. Hoshijima, knowing that Yamamura was intending to build a house, introduced him to Endo, and Endo introduced him to Wright. A wooden tag, or *munafuda*, was found by some university students recording the date of the placement of the ridgepost as 11 February 1924 and the designer/supervisor as Arato Endo. The contractor was noted as Mera Komulen. Though it was designed in 1918, it cannot have been built until later.

In 1974, the house was designated an Important Cultural Landmark. It was the first such designation of a building from the Tashido Era (1912-26). c85

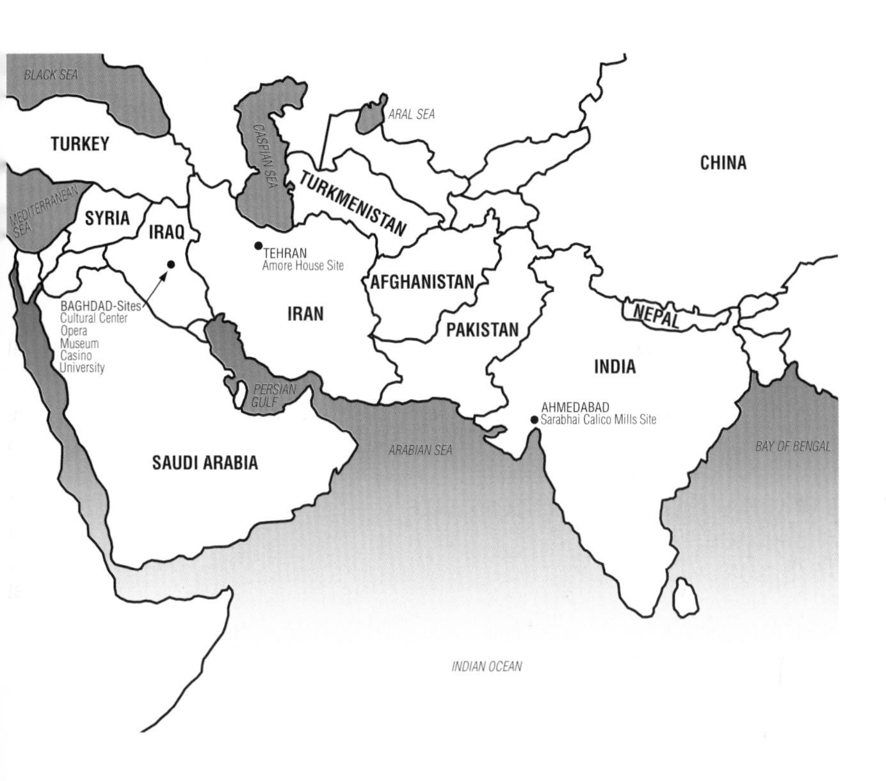

■ Few people are aware that Wright produced designs for this region. None of them was constructed, but his work did result in two buildings being built by Wright's successor firm, Taliesin Associated Architects, in Baghdad. Despite Wright's popularity in Europe, his Middle Eastern and southern Asian projects were greater in number than his European ones. His sole design for Europe is his 1953 proposal for the Masieri Memorial in Venice.

MIDDLE EASTERN AND SOUTH ASIAN SITES

See map on p135 for locations.

AMORE HOUSE SITE
Tehran, Iran
1957 5801

■ There is very little information about this project. It is similar in form to the Millard House of Pasadena (p61), and may also have been intended to have been built in concrete or concrete block.

CULTURAL CENTER, OPERA HOUSE, MUSEUM, KIOSKS, CASINO AND UNIVERSITY SITES, Baghdad, Iraq
1957 5748

■ The first commission was for the Opera House with its circular ramp for car parking. This project, however, expanded to include a civic auditorium, and planetarium for the King of Iraq, Faisal II. The university was to be located on the other river bank in the center of the city. Wright visited Baghdad in May 1957. The following year, the King who was born in 1935, and crowned in 1939, aged four, was overthrown and executed. Drawings exist in the archives of the Frank Lloyd Foundation for each phase of the Baghdad designs.

SARABHAI CALICO MILL STORE SITE
Ahmedabad, India
1945 4508

■ The Gautam Sarabhai family whose company commissioned the design had a son apprenticed at Taliesin. The intention was to build a department store that would extend the family cotton mill business into retail, selling cotton fabrics. The multi-storied building was not air conditioned but had a central open courtyard. The complicated use of natural air conditioning and engineering was beyond what could be understood by the local contractors at the time and the project was abandoned.

The store was to be built on Kalupur Relief Road in Ahmedabad, India, on a small site that was only 60 feet square. The first letter to Wright concerning the project was from Mr JA Ghandi with offices in 30 Rockefeller Plaza, RCA Building, New York. Besides the obvious fabrics that the company made, the store was to sell toilet articles, soaps, hair oils, sugar, candies and pharmaceuticals. It was to include a bookshop, a parlor for selling paintings and art, and a restaurant with garden terrace on the top or sixth floor. All of its stock was to be produced by subsidiaries of the company in India and in East Africa; the company's head office was in London. The cost was estimated at about $120,000. Mr Gautam Sarabhai, the chairman of the company, visited Wright at Taliesin in the early summer of 1946.

Arizona

Arizona Biltmore Hotel, Phoenix, Arizona 85016. The hotel is available at any time with a room or restaurant reservation. There are several first-class restaurants in the hotel. Call 602/955-6600.

Grady Gammage Memorial Auditorium, Tempe, Arizona 85281. Regular performances are scheduled in the auditorium during the season. Call 602/965-4050.

Southwest Christian Seminary, Phoenix, Arizona 80513. Call 602/246-9206 for information on regular services.

Taliesin West, Scottsdale, Arizona 85261. There are regular tours. These are in the mornings during the summer. Call 602/860-8810.

California

Anderton Court Shops, Beverly Hills, California 90210.The businesses are open during regular office hours. There are open spaces between the offices that one may walk through.

Aline Barnsdall House (Hollyhock House) Los Angeles 90027. Regular tours are available.

Charles Ennis House, Los Angeles 90027. Special events and tours are available. Call 213/660-0607.

Samuel Freeman House, Los Angeles, California 90028. USC owns the Freeman House and it is operated by the School of Architecture. The building is in poor condition. Public access is not available in the foreseeable future.

Paul Hanna (Honeycomb) House, Stanford, California 94305. An extensive restoration program is due for completion in summer1999 and tours are expected to be given thereafter. Contact Stanford University for additional information.

Marin County Civic Center, San Rafael, California 94903. The center is open during regular business hours. Tours are also available, call 415/499-7407.

Morris Gift Shop, San Francisco, California 94108. The shop is open during business hours.

Pilgrim Congregational Church, Redding, California 96001. There are no special tours, but the church is open during services.

Iowa

George C Stockman House, Mason City, Iowa 50401. Regular tours are available. Call 515/423-1923 or the McNeider Museum.

Lowell Walter House & River Pavilion, Quasqueton, Iowa 52326. Regular tours are available. Call 319/934-3572.

Missouri

City National Bank & Hotel, Mason City, Iowa 50401. There are no interior public spaces as it no longer functions as a bank or hotel.

Henry J Allen House, Wichita, Kansas 67208. The house is open for special tours. Call 316/687-1027.

Community Christian Church, Kansas City, Missouri 64112. The church is open for regular services. Call 816/561-6531.

Montana

Lockridge Medical Clinic, Whitefish, Montana 59937. This building is now a bank and is open during normal business hours.

Oklahoma

Price Tower, Bartlesville, Oklahoma 74003. The building is undergoing a change of ownership and use. Tours available. Call 918/661-7417.

Texas

Kalita Humphries Theater, Dallas Theater Center. Regular performances are scheduled during the season.

Japan

Jiyu Gakuen School of the Free Spirit, Tokyo, Japan. The building is undergoing a three-year restoration program and will be open for tours in 2002.

Imperial Hotel, Tokyo (original site). The new building is one of the finest hotels in the world with several fine restaurants and the original 1923 bar.

Meiji-mura Museum (reconstruction of the Imperial Hotel). The park is open every day. Call (0568) 67-0314.

Tazaemon Yamamura House, Ashiya, Japan. This house had considerable damage in the Kobe earthquake and has been repaired and is open for special tours. It is open to the public on Wednesdays, Saturdays, Sundays and national Japanese holidays from 10am to 4pm. Call (0797) 38-1720 or the Yodogawa Steel Company on (06) 245-1720.

ACKNOWLEDGMENTS

■ I would like to thank everyone mentioned in this collection of short narratives, and many others who have assisted me in my research. My first introduction to the West was on a trip with Gay Anderson Pearson. She was quite gracious and most helpful in all regards. I appreciate all of her help over many years. I was commissioned to photograph the Yosemite Valley for a book by Walter Creese, one of my former professors from the University of Illinois, Urbana. Gay and I then drove to the Los Angeles area, where I visited Charles Eames at his office and met Page Reinse, Editor-in-Chief of *Architectural Digest* at a dinner for three at the Storer House along with the owner, Dr Jacobi. As a result of this meeting, Ms Rense agreed to begin the *Architectural Digest*'s Historic Architecture and Gardens features. I wrote the first Historic Architecture article on Mackintosh's Hill House and several others, including the one on the Ennis House. I met Randell Makinson, Director of the Gamble House in Pasadena. The program that he had initiated had already been copied by the Chicago Architecture Foundation, and as a member of the Board of Directors of the Frank Lloyd Wright Home and Studio Foundation in Oak Park, Don Kalec and I went to discuss the docent training program and his archive and library plans. We also visited Lloyd and Eric Wright, and paid a visit to an ailing Catherine Wright in Santa Barbara. We were able to interview John Lloyd Wright's widow at their house. Gay then flew back to Chicago when Don and I flew to Phoenix, and I saw Taliesin West for the first time. Phoenix in August can be quite hot. We met with many of the apprentices and interviewed several of them. David and Gladys Wright graciously welcomed us and patiently answered all our questions. This trip set the stage for many others over the next twenty-five years.

Randell Makinson, now Director Emeritus of The Gamble House, became a close friend and shared his experiences and research with me. He also introduced me to his many friends that were also interested in Wright and in architecture. Randell's guidance and counsel have proved invaluable. Thank you, Randell. Among them, and first on the list, were Ginny and Gene Kazor. Ginny had just become the Director of the Hollyhock House and Gene was doing a lot of impressive woodwork. Ginny has been so helpful and supportive over many years. I am only saddened that Gene passed away several years ago. Edmund Teske was introduced to me by Ginny. Edmund recounted stories of his time at Taliesin, as official photographer, and his beginnings in Chicago, as well as how he found Aline Barnsdall dead in Residence B. He worked with me on two very long articles on his work and life for *The Frank Lloyd Wright Newsletter*. I regret that Edmund has passed away.

Gus Brown had recently bought the Ennis House and kindly allowed me to photograph the unusual art glass. Joel Silver is the second owner of the Storer House. He invited me to the house while it was undergoing a major restoration program under his direction. We became friends and I stayed at the house several times during the mid-1980s. Sam and Harriett Freeman, and later Jeff Chusid, have been all been wonderful in allowing me access to study the Freeman House. Jim and Janeen Marin, who both have considerable experience in design, and have one of the finest Arts and Crafts collections in the world, containing several Wright items, have also been very generous. Jack Larsen was very helpful with information on his house.

Kathryn Smith has always answered all my questions and put me on to many new things. Bob Winter personally and through his books on California architecture provided a considerable amount of information. The Getty Museum's staff, Bred Swerdlow, Mark Henderson, and Wim De Wit, have made their collection of Wright materials available to me and answered my many questions.

Diane Kanner's interest and information have been very helpful.

Masami and Yoshiko Tanigawa have toured the states many times with pilgrims from Japan and I have met with them not only on their Chicago stop, but also in San Francisco and Los Angeles. They went out of their way to help to arrange an elaborate tour for me throughout Japan. They took me to every site of a Wright design and many shrines and sites that Wright is known to have visited on his travels. They have answered my many questions on the Japanese work as well as discussing all of Wright's work. I owe them very much for all of their help and friendship over the last twenty-five years.

Paul and Jean Hanna invited me to stay with them many times. Paul Turner and Bob Hoergen have filled in many gaps and kept me informed of more recent developments.

Tom Rickard of Tacoma has been a source of considerable information and assistance. He has delved into details with exacting precision and voluminous footnotes. No question was beyond his range and depth. His help is much appreciated. Milton Stricker has also assisted with this book.

Debra Vick of Seattle and the Tracys showed me their beautiful homes. I am sorry I was not able to stay longer and enjoy the experiences.

Bob Sweeney has always been an exacting scholar and this work is reflected in every publication authored by him. Many of us wish he would publish a second volume of his useful and famous bibliography. He has always been gracious in his assistance with any investigation.

Art Neff and his wife have been enthusiastic in joining in the search. Wallace Neff Jr has answered my questions about his memories about Wright and his father.

Paul Crist lectured several times about the importance of these investigations and helped many times. Lloyd Oberman moved from Los Angeles to Madison, Wisconsin, but was always interested in our investigations.

All the people from the Gamble House – Jean, Nancy and Bob Ullrich, Doris Gertmanian – were so helpful and gracious the many, many times I was staying at the beautiful Gamble House. Bob and Judy Kopulos, who were clients when they owned their Wright house, are due special thanks for their warm hospitality.

The late Mrs Wright, the late Wes Peters, Bruce Pfeiffer, Charles and Minerva Montooth, Tony Putnam, Ling Po, Dr Joe Roark, David Dodge, John DeKoven Hill, the late Dick Carney, Oscar Munoz, Margo Stipe, Penny Fowler, Susan Lockart and many others at Taliesin made me feel welcome for many years, and were always willing to share their lives and remembrances with me. Thank you very much.

Aaron Green shared his vast knowledge. Rich Branom introduced me to Mr Kraus and provided other useful information. David and Gladys Wright were most gracious in allowing my students to explore their beautiful house. They have warmly hosted my many visits. I certainly enjoy them both. Elizabeth Wright Ingraham and the late Anne Baxter, both granddaughters of Wright, were always lots of fun in retelling the family stories. Eric and Lloyd Wright hosted several visits in Lloyd's Los Angeles studio.

Mrs Berger and Dr Walton have spent valuable time on the phone answering my many questions and inquires. Betty Noble, the daughter of Elizabeth Noble, has collected the amazing story of her family and made it available to me. Dr Robert McCoy of Mason City, Iowa has provided me with a considerable amount of information about Mr Stockman. He lives in a wonderful Walter Burley Griffin and was very helpful in my undergraduate thesis on Griffin at the University of Illinois.

Robert Lynn Ooley, architect of Carpinteria, California, provided the information about George C Stewart and the house. Thank you. George M Goodwin made his considerable collection available. He was always willing to explore new areas.

Bruce & Yoshiko Smith and their daughter put me up in their Berkeley apartment and helped to teach me to use the PageMaker software. Brian Spencer of Phoenix has lent his knowledge and encouragement for twenty-five years. There is now a five-year plan in place with his wife Pam. Jon Jepson, Carl Witte and Linda Pate Laird of Davis & Shaw in Denver have always offered support for these efforts. I am grateful to Christine Bee, Librarian of the Murphy Memorial Library in Monona, Iowa, for information on the Meiers, as I am to the many reference librarians from most of the towns that contain Wright buildings. I owe much to their research efforts on my behalf. Don Hensman made many long and occasionally, dangerous journeys with me to the north country. Thanks Don.

Thank you, John Stoddart, Maggie Toy, Andrea Bettella and Helen Castle for all the help and guidance.

I also owe my thanks to my family, who have become a bit more interested in Frank Lloyd Wright, and Ann Terando, who now has several Wright stories of her own.

BOOKS

■ Frank Lloyd Wright, *The Story of the Tower: The Tree that Escaped the Crowded Forest*, Horizon Press (New York), 1956.
This was the first monograph produced on a single Wright building. After a short essay, there is a series of construction photographs by Harold Price Sr's son, Joe Price. It is this that makes the book so invaluable today.

■ Hessell Tiltman, *The Imperial Hotel Story*, 1964.
A double-page fold out book by a newspaper reporter, who was a Japanese correspondent from 1935, and was often in residence at the hotel. Much of the information in this sixty-two-page book is not available elsewhere. It gives what a reporter would look for – the who, what, when, where and why of the hotel.

■ Cary James, *The Imperial Hotel*, Charles A Tuttle Co (Vermont), 1968.
Published the year that the hotel was demolished, this book is by Cary, a San Francisco Bay area architect and member of the AIA.

■ Antonin Raymond, *An Autobiography*, Charles A Tuttle Co (Rutland, Vermont & Tokyo), 1973.
This book tells Raymond's life story. He worked with Wright on several projects at Taliesin and then accompanied Wright to Japan, where he worked on the Imperial Hotel. Raymond stayed on in Japan establishing his own successful independent practice.

■ David Gebhard, Roger Montgomery, Robert Winter, John Woodbridge, Sally Woodbridge and Peregrine Smith, *A Guide to Architecture in San Francisco & Northern California*, Peregrine Smith (Salt Lake City), 1973.
A full listing of all architecturally significant buildings in the northern California.

■ Stanley Marcus, *Minding The Store*, Little Brown & Co (New York), 1974.
This is Stanley Marcus's autobiography, largely centered on the Neiman-Marcus store and his family. It includes several pages about the design of his Wright house. He knew Burton Tremaine of the Meteor Crater project and Elizabeth Arden,

■ John Sergeant, *Frank Lloyd Wright's Usonian Houses*, Whitney Library of Design-Watson/Guptil (New York), 1976.
One wishes that the book were two or three times longer and included more of Wright's buildings and projects. What it contains is very useful.

■ David Gebhard and Robert Winter, *A Guide to Architecture in Los Angeles & Southern California*, Peregrine Smith (Salt Lake City), 1977.
A comprehensive listing of nearly all the significant buildings in southern California. It encompasses not only Wright's buildings, but those of his two sons and former assistants.

■ Sylvia Linse Schmitt *(ed), Mason City, Iowa: An Architectural Heritage*, (Mason City, Iowa), 1977.
This gives a history of Mason City and its development, as well as a survey of all the important residential and commercial buildings in the city, including those by Wright, Griffin, Barry Byrne and William Drummond.

■ Robert L Sweeney, *Frank Lloyd Wright: An Annotated Bibliography*, Hennessey & Ingalls (Los Angeles), 1978.
Virtually every publication on Wright and his buildings is noted in this excellent work. There is an index by building name for those interested in more historical background. One wishes that an updated volume might be forthcoming.

■ Esther McCoy, *Vienna to Los Angeles: Two Journeys*, A+A Press (Santa Monica, California), 1979.
Rudolph Schindler, a Viennese emigré, worked for Wright during the design and construction of several of the buildings in the West.

■ *Images from Within: The Photographs of Edmund Teske*, Friends of Photography (Carmel, California), 1980
This is a rare book showing the full range of Teske's photography. It includes Taliesin West and two of the Barnsdall buildings. It is artfully presented and beautifully printed.

■ Paul R and Jean S Hanna, *Frank Lloyd Wright's Hanna House,* Architectural History Foundation (New York), 1981; second edition 1987.
A short book that covers the essential points of the design and construction of the Hanna House. There are many good photographs of the entire process including Mr Hanna making furniture in his shop.

■ Robert T Ray and Lois Rutledge, *Trails West to Red Willow County Nebraska*, (McCook, Nebraska), 1982.
A detailed book on the families and individuals that lived and worked in the county, including a long narrative on Harvey P Sutton.

■ Anthony Alofsin (ed), *Frank Lloyd Wright: An Index to the Taliesin Correspondence*, Garland Press (New York), 1983.
The microfilmed letters to and from Frank Lloyd Wright are indexed and cross indexed within these five volumes. Bruce Brooks Pfeiffer, the Director of Archives at Taliesin, has compiled the definitive list of all of Frank Lloyd Wright's work. This list would be even more valuable if it were updated and published separately.

■ Walter L Creese, *The Crowning of the American Landscape: Eight Great Spaces and Their Buildings*, Princeton University Press, 1985.

■ Bruce Brooks Pfeiffer, *Treasures of Taliesin: Seventy-Six Unbuilt Designs*, Southern Illinois University Press (Carbondale, Illinois), 1985.
Short commentaries on these projects reveal information about the clients and their buildings. Short stories of the project and client are included with beautiful pencil drawings.

■ Bette Koprivila Pappas, *Frank Lloyd Wright: No Passing Fancy, A Pictorial History*, self-published, 1985.
A very expressive essay, which details and accompanies many photos of the Pappas House during and after the construction.

■ Henry Whiting II and Robert G Waite, *Teater's Knoll*, Norwood Press (Midland, Michigan), 1987.
This is the complete history of the design, construction and reconstruction of this small artist's studio in Idaho.

■ David Gebhard, *Romanza: the California Architecture of Frank Lloyd Wright*, Chronicle Books (San Francisco), 1988.
Short notes accompany photos of Wright's California buildings.

■ Donald Hoffmann, *Frank Lloyd Wright's Hollyhock House*, Dover (New York), 1992.
A concise and complete history of Aline Barnsdall and the Hollyhock House. There is, however, little information about the other buildings that were built at the site such as Residences A and B. Perhaps they will be included in the second edition of this well written book.

■ Scott Zimmerman, *Guide to Frank Lloyd Wright's California*, Gibbs Smith (Salt Lake City), 1992.
A guide with maps, directions and a little information about the California buildings.

■ Kathryn Smith, *Frank Lloyd Wright: Hollyhock House and Olive Hill: Buildings and Projects for Aline Barnsdall*, Rizzoli (New York), 1992.
All of the work Wright designed for Aline Barnsdall is detailed in this wonderful work. It is one of the very best expositions and analyses of any of Wright's projects.

■ Anthony Alofsin, *Frank Lloyd Wright: The Lost Years, 1910-1922*, University of Chicago Press (Chicago), 1993.
Many important derails of Wright's work in California and Japan, and elsewhere, are detailed in this excellent book that focuses on a twelve-year period in Wright's career. It is the product of a tremendous amount of research. Any sequels, like 1922 to 1932, would be welcome.

■ Davis Gebhard and Gerald Mansheim, *Buildings of Iowa* by Society of Architectural Historians, Oxford University Press (New York), 1993.
This is an early volume of what will become the first comprehensive listing of all buildings of note in the US. It is arranged geographically and by city. Maps are included where there are clusters of buildings. It needs to have many more

■ Norman M and Dorothy K Karasick, *The Oilman's Daughter: A Biography of Aline Barnsdall*, Carleston Publishing (Encino, California), 1993.
This book starts with the oil fortunes acquired by Aline Barnsdall's father and grandfather, and traces her life through the social causes she championed. There are several chapters on the Hollyhock House and its associated buildings.

■ Kevin Nute, *Frank Lloyd Wright and Japan*, Van Nostrand Reinhold (New York), 1993.
The network of people that assisted Wright with Japanese prints and fed his appetite for Japanese art and life is explored here. The book also tries to deal with the influences of Japanese architectural design on his buildings. It does not, however, investigate in detail Wright's designs for Japan.

■ William Allin Storrer, *The Frank Lloyd Wright Companion*, University of Chicago Press (Chicago and London), 1993.
A considerable amount of work went into the assembly of this book. Plans for every Wright building ever built are included. Storrer has included much information on many little known clients.

■ Judith Dunham, *Details of Frank Lloyd Wright: The California Work 1909-1974*, Chronicle Books (San Francisco), 1994.
There are many close-up color photos of Wright's California works and essays on each building.

■ David Gebhard, and Robert Winter, *Los Angeles: An Architectural Guide*, Gibbs Smith (Salt Lake City), 1994.
A good guide to nearly all of the interesting and worthwhile buildings in Los Angeles and surrounding suburbs. One wishes for more photographs in a book like this. The index lists buildings under the designers but not individually.

■ Robert L Sweeney, *Wright in Hollywood*, Architectural History Foundation/MIT Press (Cambridge, Mass), 1994.
This book covers the buildings Wright designed during his Hollywood era, and includes those for Arizona. It brings together new information about many well known and lesser known buildings and projects.

■ Masami Tanigawa, *Measured Drawings of Wright's Japanese Work*, Shokokusha Publishing Co (Tokyo, Japan), 1995.
This great book gives all the information known on Wright's Japanese buildings. It includes measured drawings of the plans and wall elevations, as well as furniture and other decorative arts. The book covers the built and the proposed projects.

■ Robert Eason, *Dallas Theater Center: The Early Years, 1955-1982*, 1996.
This is a privately published soft-cover book from the Dallas Public Library on the short history of the building and the group. It includes biographical sketches on Humphries, Wright and Baker.

■ Melanie Birk (ed), *Frank Lloyd Wright's Fifty Views of Japan: The 1905 Photo Album,* Pomegranate Artbooks (Rohnert Park, California), 1996
This book includes several essays by Anthony Alofsin, Masami Tanigawa, Jack Quinan and Kevin Nute. It discusses Wright's first Japanese trip through the fifty-five photographs that Wright took while he was there.

■ Shinji Hata, *Frank Lloyd Wright and Japan*, Stichting Siebold Council (Tokyo, Japan), 1997.
This book accompanies the traveling exhibition about Wright that toured Japan. It covers many of the Japanese folding screens that were built in at Taliesin and Taliesin West, as well as many other pieces. The screens were recently restored and will be returned to their original locations.

PERIODICALS

■ Jenkin Lloyd Jones, 'A House for a Cousin: The Richard Lloyd Jones House,' *Frank Lloyd Wright Newsletter*, vol 2, no 4, Fourth Quarter 1979, pp1-3.
Written by the son of the original client and a relative of Wright's, the article discusses the design from a personal standpoint and notes the subsequent owners and their stewardship.

■ Masami Tanigawa, 'Motion Picture Theater-Tokyo,' *Frank Lloyd Wright Newsletter*, vol 2, no 4, Fourth Quarter 1979, pp8-9.
A discussion of the theater which includes new information, a photo of the plaster model and selected details.

■ Masami Tanigawa, 'The Odawara Hotel,' *Frank Lloyd Wright Newsletter*, vol 3, no 1, First Quarter 1980, pp12-13.
This is the first article to suggest that the Odawara Hotel may have begun construction.

■ Stephen D Helmer, 'Grady Gammage Auditorium and the Baghdad Opera Project: Two Late Designs by Frank Lloyd Wright,' *Frank Lloyd Wright Newsletter*, vol 3, no 4, Fourth Quarter 1980, pp10-17.
This well-illustrated article discusses the similarities in design between two projects that were executed at a similar date.

■ Delton Ludwig, 'Frank Lloyd Wright in the Bitter Root Valley of Montana,' *Frank Lloyd Wright Newsletter*, vol 5, no. 2, Second Quarter 1982, pp6-15.
A complete discussion of Como Orchards, Bitter Root Inn and the town of Bitter Root. This well researched article is illustrated with useful plans and photographs.

■ Paul R and Jean S Hanna, 'Furnishing our Frank Lloyd Wright Home,' *Frank Lloyd Wright Newsletter*, vol 5, no 2, Second Quarter 1982, pp1-6.
This article could be considered another chapter to the book, *A Client's Report*, that the Hannas wrote detailing the design and construction of their famous house.

THIS IS A FULL LIST OF THE PROPOSED, EXISTING AND DEMOLISHED BUILDINGS THAT APPEAR IN THE FLW FIELD GUIDES.

Volume Name	Upper Great Lakes	West	East	MetroChicago
Key	UGL	W	E	MC

	Vol	Date	Opus	Page
Ablin, George, Bakersfield, Calif.	**W**	**1958**	**5812**	**45**
Adams, Harry S, Oak Park, Ill.	MC	1913	1301	81
Adams, Mary MW, Highland Park, Ill.	MC	1905	0501	21
Adams, William, Chicago, Ill.	MC	1900	0001	127
Adelman, Albert, Fox Point, Wisc.	UGL	1948	4801	78
Adelman, Benjamin, Phoenix, Ariz.	**W**	**1951**	**5101**	**77**
Affleck, Gregor S, Bloomfield Hills, Mich.	UGL	1940	4111	115
Airplane House – see Gilmore.	UGL	1908	0806	57
Allen, Henry J, Wichita, Kansas.	**W**	**1917**	**1701**	**91**
Allentown Art Museum, Little House Library.	E	1912	1304	
Alpaugh, Amy, Northport, Mich.	UGL	1947	4703	99
Alsop, Caroll, Oskaloosa, Iowa.	**W**	**1948**	**4804**	**113**
Amberg, JH, Grand Rapids, Mich.	UGL	1910	1001	106
American Embassy, Tokyo, Japan, site.	**W**	**1914**	**1406**	**132**
American Systems Buildings – Richards.	UGL	1916	1606	79
Richards, Duplex Apartments, Milwaukee, Wisc.	UGL	1916	1605	80
Richards, Small House, Milwaukee, Wisc.	UGL	1916	1605	81
American Systems, Bungalow,				
Hunt, Stephen MB, Oshkosh, Wisc.	UGL	1917	1703	35
O'Connor, JJ, Wilmette, Ill.	MC	1916	1506	37
Richards, Milwaukee, Wisc.	UGL	1916	1605	82
Vanderkloot, William J, Lake Bluff, Ill.	MC	1916	1506	18
American Systems Two-Story House,				
Burhans-Ellinwood & Co, Chicago, Ill.	MC	1917	1506	129
Hanney & Son, Evanston, Ill.	MC	1916	1506	38
Hyde, Howard H, Chicago, Ill.	MC	1917	1506	130
Meier, Delbert W, Monona, Iowa.	**W**	**1916**	**1506**	**107**
Wynant, Wilber, Gary, Ind.	MC	1917	1506	109
Amore House, Tehran, Iran, site.	**W**	**1958**	**5801**	**136**
Anderton Court, Los Angeles, Beverly Hills, Calif.	**W**	**1952**	**5032**	**50**
Angster, Herbert, Lake Bluff, Ill, site.	MC	1911	1101	18

Annunciation Greek Orthodox Church, Wauwatosa, Wisc.	UGL	1956	5611	83
Anthony, Howard E, Benton Harbor, Mich.	UGL	1949	4901	131
Arden, Elizabeth, Desert Spa, Phoenix, Ariz, site.	**W**	**1945**	**4506**	**78**
Arizona Biltmore Hotel, Phoenix, Ariz.	**W**	**1927**	**2710**	**74**
Arizona State Capitol, Phoenix, Ariz, site.	**W**	**1957**	**5732**	**78**
Armstrong, Andrew F, Ogden Dunes, Ind.	MC	1939	3901	111
Arnold, E Clarke, Columbus, Wisc.	UGL	1954	5401	66
Auldbrass, Stevens Plantation, Yemassee, SC.	E	1940	4015	
Austin, Charlcey, Greenville, SC.	E	1951	5102	
Bach, Emil, Chicago, Ill.	MC	1915	1501	115
Baghdad Projects, Iraq, site.	**W**	**1957**	**5748**	**136**
Bagley, Frederick, Hinsdale, Ill.	MC	1894	9401	101
Bagley, Joseph J, Grand Beach, Mich.	UGL	1916	1601	134
Bailleres, Raul, Acapulco, Mexico, site.	**W**	**1952**	**5202**	**123**
Baird, Theodore, Amherst, Mass.	E	1940	4001	
Baker, Frank J, Wilmette, Ill.	MC	1909	0901	36
Balch, Oscar B, Oak Park, Ill.	MC	1911	1102	80
Baldwin, Hiram, Kenilworth, Ill.	MC	1905	0502	35
Banff National Park Pavilion, Alberta, Canada, site.	**W**	**1911**	**1302**	**121**
Bannerstone House – see Dana, Susan Lawrence.	E	1904	9905	
Barnsdall, Aline (Hollyhock House), L. A., Calif.	**W**	**1917**	**1705**	**56**
Barton, George, Buffalo, NY.	E	1903	0301	
Bassett, Dr HW, Oak Park, Ill, site.	MC	1894	9402	74
Bazett, Sidney, Hillsborough, Calif.	**W**	**1940**	**4002**	**32**
Beach Cottages, Egypt, site.	E	1927	2711	
Beachy, Peter A, Oak Park, Ill.	MC	1906	0601	72
Berger, Robert, San Anselmo, Calif.	**W**	**1950**	**5039**	**24**
Beth Sholom Synagogue, Elkins Park, Penn.	E	1954	5313	
Bitter Root Valley Sites, Darby, Mont.				
Bitter Root Inn, Darby, Montana, site.	**W**	**1909**	**0918**	**65**
Town Plan, Darby, Montana, site.	**W**	**1909**	**0926**	**65**
Blair, Quintin, Cody, Wyoming.	**W**	**1952**	**5203**	**67**
Blossom, George, Chicago, Ill.	MC	1892	9201	123
Bogk, Frederick C, Milwaukee, Wisc.	UGL	1916	1602	85
Boomer, Jorgine, Phoenix, Ariz.	**W**	**1953**	**5302**	**76**
Booth, Sherman, House, Glencoe, Ill.	MC	1915	1502	26

Cottage.	MC	1911	1119	32
Ravine Bluffs Development, housing.	MC	1916	1505	25
Lot 10: Perry, Charles R.	MC	1915	1516	27
Lot 15: Ellis, C J (Kier, William F).	MC	1915	1605	29
Lot 16: Finch, Frank (Ross, William F).	MC	1915	1516	30
Lot 17, Compton, J M (Kissam, Lute F).	MC	1915	1516	31
Lot 22, Gilfillan, S J (Root, Hollis R).	MC	1915	1516	28
Borah, Al, Barrington Hills, Ill. Erdman Prefab.	MC	1957	5518	47
Boswell, William P, Indian Hill, Ohio.	E	1957	5704	
Bott, Frank, Kansas City, Mo.	**W**	**1956**	**5627**	**116**
Boulter, Cedric G, Cincinnati, Ohio.	E	1954	5403	
Boynton, Edward E, Rochester, NY.	E	1908	0801	
Bradley, R Harley, Kankakee, Ill.	E	1900	0002	
Bramson Dress Shop, Oak Park, Ill, site.	MC	1937	3706	74
Brandes, Ray Z, Issaquah, Washington.	**W**	**1952**	**5204**	**18**
Brauner, Erling, Okemos, Mich.	UGL	1948	4601	109
Brigham, Edmund F, Glencoe, Ill.	MC	1915	1503	34
Brown, Charles A, Evanston, Ill.	MC	1905	0503	39
Brown, Eric V, Kalamazoo, Mich.	UGL	1959	5003	127
Brownes Bookstore, Chicago, site.	MC	1907	0802	134
Bubilian, AH, Rochester, Minn.	UGL	1947	4709	29
Buehler, Maynard P, Orinda, Calif.	**W**	**1948**	**4805**	**30**
Burhans-Ellinwod & Co, Chicago, Ill.	MC	1917	1506	129
Burleigh see O'Connor, JJ, Wilmette, Ill.	MC	1916	1506	37
Calico Mill Store see Sarabhai, Ahmedabad, India, site.	**W**	**1945**	**4508**	**136**
Carlson, Raymond, Phoenix, Ariz.	**W**	**1950**	**5004**	**73**
Carr, John O, Glenview, Ill.	MC	1950	5014	48
Carr, WS, Grand Beach, Mich.	UGL	1916	1603	133
Cass, William, New York City, Staten Island, NY.	E	1959	5518	
Chahroudi, AK, Lake Mahopac, New York, NY.	E	1951	5104	
Charnley, James, Chicago, Ill.	MC	1891	9001	132
Ocean Springs, Miss.	E	1890	9101	
Cheney, Edwin H, Oak Park, Ill.	MC	1904	0401	84
Christian, John E, West Lafayette, Ind.	E	1954	5405	
Christie, James B, Bernardsville, NJ.	E	1940	4003	
Cinema, San Diego, Calif, site.	**W**	**1905**	**0517**	**43**

Circle Pines Resort, Cloverdale, Mich, site.	UGL	1942	4205	119
City National Bank & Hotel, Mason City, Iowa.	**W**	**1909**	**0902**	**104**
Claremont Hotel, Berkeley, Calif, site.	**W**	**1957**	**5709**	**29**
Clark, George, Carmel, Calif, site.	**W**	**1951**	**5112**	**38**
Clark, W Irving, La Grange, Ill.	MC	1893	9209	103
Community Christian Church, Kansas City, Mo.	**W**	**1940**	**4004**	**118**
Como Orchards Cottages, Darby, Mont.	**W**	**1910**	**1002**	**66**
Compton, JM, Lot 17, Ravine Bluffs, Glencoe.	MC	1915	1516	31
Cooke, Andrew, Virginia Beach, Virginia.	E	1953	5219	
Coonley, Avery, Riverside, Ill.	MC	1908	0803	91
Coonley Playhouse, Riverside, Ill.	MC	1912	1201	93
Copeland, William H, Oak Park, Ill.	MC	1909	0904	66
Crosbyton Schoolhouse, Texas, site.	**W**	**1900**	**0012**	**101**
Cudney, Ralph & Wellington, Chandler, Ariz, site.	**W**	**1927**	**2706**	**83**
Crystal Heights, Washington DC, site.	E	1939	4016	
Cummings Real Estate, River Forest, Ill, site.	MC	1907	0702	58
Currier Art Gallery, Zimmerman House, Manchester, NH.	E	1950	5214	
Dallas Theater Center, Dallas, Texas.	**W**	**1955**	**5514**	**98**
Dana, Susan Lawrence, Springfield, Ill.	E	1904	9905	
Daphne Funeral Home, San Francisco, site.	**W**	**1945**	**4823**	**29**
Darby Plan, Montana, site.	**W**	**1909**	**0926**	**65**
Davenport, E Arthur, River Forest, Ill.	MC	1901	0101	57
Davidson, Walter V, Buffalo, NY.	E	1908	0804	
Davis, Richard, Marion, Indiana.	E	1950	5037	
Death Valley, Calif, Johnson Desert Compound, site.	**W**	**1921**	**2306**	**41**
Deephaven – see Little, Francis W.	UGL	1913	1304	137
Library, Allentown, Penn.	E	1912	1304	
Metropolitan Museum, New York, NY.	E	1912	1304	
Deertrack – see Roberts, Abby.	UGL	1936	3603	97
DeRhodes, KC, South Bend, Ind.	E	1906	0602	
Dobkins, John J, Canton, Ohio.	E	1954	5407	
Doheny Ranch Project, Beverly Hills, site.	**W**	**1923**	**2104**	**51**
Donahoe Triptych, Phoenix, Ariz, site.	**W**	**1959**	**5901**	**78**
Duncan, Don, Lisle, Ill.	MC	1957	5518	99
Edwards, James, Okemos, Mich.	UGL	1949	4904	110
Elam, SP, Austin, Minn.	UGL	1951	5105	30

Ellis, CJ, Lot 15, Ravine Bluffs, Glencoe, Ill.	MC	1915	1516	28
Emmond, Robert G, La Grange, Ill.	MC	1892	9202	104
Ennis, Charles, Los Angeles, Calif.	**W**	**1924**	**2401**	**55**
Erdman Prefab houses, Upper Great Lakes,				
Iber, Frank, Plover, Wisc.	UGL	1957	5518	34
Jackson, Arnold, Madison.	UGL	1957	5518	67
La Fond, St Joseph, Minn.	UGL	1960	5518	20
McBean, James, Rochester, Minn.	UGL	1957	5706	27
Mollica, Joseph, Bayside, Wisc.	UGL	1958	5518	77
Rudin, Walter, Madison.	UGL	1957	5706	61
Van Tamlen, Eugene, Madison.	UGL	1956	5518	60
Erdman Prefab houses, MetroChicago,				
Borah, Al, Barrington Hills, Ill.	MC	1957	5518	47
Duncan, Don, Lisle, Ill.	MC	1957	5518	99
Erdman Prefab houses. East,				
Cass, William, New York City, NY.	E	1959	5518	
Zaferiou, Socrates, Blauvelt, NY.	E	1961	5518	
Eppstein, Samuel, Galesburg, Mich.	UGL	1949	4905	121
Euchtman, Joseph, Baltimore, Maryland.	E	1940	4005	
Evans, Raymond W, Chicago, Ill.	MC	1908	0805	128
Exhibition House, New York City, NY, site.	E	1953	5314	
E-Z Polish Factory, Chicago, Ill.	MC	1905	0504	117
Fabyan, George, Geneva, Ill.	MC	1907	0703	96
Fallingwater – see Kaufmann, Edgar.	E	1936	3602	
Fasbender Medical Clinic, Hastings, Minn.	UGL	1957	5730	26
Fawcett, Randall, Los Banos, Calif.	**W**	**1955**	**5418**	**40**
Feiman, Ellis A, Canton, Ohio.	E	1954	5408	
Finch, Frank B, Lot 16, Ravine Bluffs, Glencoe, Ill.	MC	1915	1516	30
Fir Tree, Friedman, Pecos, NM.	**W**	**1952**	**4512**	**88**
First Christian Church, Phoenix, Ariz.	W	1950	5033	72
Florida Southern College: Lakeland, Fla.,	E	1938	3805	
Administration Building.	E	1945	3805	
Danforth Chapel.	E	1954	3805	
Industrial Arts Building.	E	1942	3805	
Pfeiffer Chapel.	E	1938	3805	
Roux Library.	E	1941	3805	

Science Building.	E	1953	3805	
Seminar Buildings.	E	1940	3805	
Fountainhead, Hughes, Jackson, Miss.	E	1949	4908	
Foster, Stephen A, Chicago, Ill.	MC	1900	0003	131
Fox River Country Club, Geneva, Ill, site.	MC	1907	0704	96
Francis Apartments, Chicago, Ill, site.	MC	1895	9501	121
Francisco Terrace, Oak Park (formerly Chicago), site.	MC	1895	9502	89
Frederick, Louis B, Barrington Hills, Ill.	MC	1954	5426	46
Freeman, Samuel, Los Angeles, Calif.	**W**	**1924**	**2402**	**54**
Freeman, Warren H, Hinsdale, Ill.	MC	1903	0312	100
Freund y Cia Dep. Store, San Salvador, El Salvador, site.	**W**	**1955**	**5425**	**123**
Fricke, William G, Oak Park, Ill.	MC	1901	0201	85
Friedman, Allan, Bannockburn, Ill.	MC	1959	5624	20
Friedman, Arnold, Pecos, NM.	**W**	**1945**	**4512**	**88**
Friedman, Sol, Pleasantville, New York, NY.	E	1949	4906	
Fuller, Grace, Glencoe, Ill, site.	MC	1906	0603	34
Fuller, Welbie, Pass Christian, Miss, site.	E	1951	5106	
Fukuhara, Arinobu, Hakone, Kanagawa, Japan.	**W**	**1918**	**1801**	**133**
Furbeck, George, Oak Park, Ill.	MC	1897	9701	88
Furbeck, Rollin, Oak Park, Ill.	MC	1897	9801	86
Gakuen, Jiyu, School, Tokyo, Japan.	**W**	**1921**	**2101**	**127**
Gale, Thomas H, Oak Park, Ill.	MC	1892	9203	61
Gale, Summer House, Whitehall, Mich.	UGL	1897	0522	101
Gale, Laura, (Mrs Thomas H) Oak Park, Ill.	MC	1909	0905	71
Gale, Cottages, Whitehall, Mich.	UGL	1905	0502	102
Gale, Walter M, Oak Park, Ill.	MC	1893	9302	60
Galesburg Country Home Acres, Mich.	UGL	1948	4828	119
Gammage Memorial Auditorium, Tempe, Ariz.	**W**	**1959**	**5904**	**84**
German Warehouse, Richland Center, Wisc.	UGL	1915	1504	39
Gerts, George, Duplex, Whitehall, Mich.	UGL	1902	0202	104
Gerts, Walter, Cottage, Whitehall, Mich.	UGL	1902	0205	103
Gerts, Walter, River Forest, Ill.	MC	1911	1114	59
Gillin, John A, Dallas, Texas.	**W**	**1950**	**5034**	**97**
Gilfillan, SJ, Ravine Bluffs, Lot 22, Glencoe, Ill.	MC	1915	1516	28
Gilmore, Eugene A, Madison, Wisc.	UGL	1908	0806	57
Ginza, Motion Picture Theater, Tokyo, Japan, site.	**W**	**1918**	**1805**	**132**

Glasner, William A, Glencoe, Ill.	MC	1905	0505	33
Glenlloyd – see Bradley, R Harley.	E	1900	0002	
Glore, Herbert F, Lake Forest, Ill.	MC	1951	5107	19
Goan, Peter, La Grange, Ill.	MC	1893	9403	105
Goddard, Lewis H, Plymouth, Mich.	UGL	1953	5317	114
Goetsch-Winkler, Okemos, Mich.	UGL	1939	3907	108
Goodrich, Harry C, Oak Park, Ill.	MC	1896	9601	83
Gordon, Conrad E, Wilsonville, Oregon.	**W**	**1957**	**5710**	**20**
Goto, Baron, Kamakura, Japan, site.	**W**	**1921**	**2105**	**133**
Grady Gammage Auditorium, Tempe, Ariz.	**W**	**1959**	**5904**	**84**
Grant, Douglas, Cedar Rapids, Iowa.	**W**	**1946**	**4503**	**110**
Grayclff, Martin, DD, Derby, NY.	E	1927	2701	
Greek Orthodox Church, Wauwatosa, Wisc.	UGL	1956	5611	83
Green, Aaron, San Francisco, Calif, site.	**W**	**1952**	**5226**	**29**
Green, Aaron, Pittsburgh, Pa, reconstruction.	E	1952	5226	
Greenberg, Maurice, Dousman, Wisc.	UGL	1954	5409	75
Greene, William B, Aurora, Ill.	MC	1912	1203	98
Gridley, AW, Batavia, Ill.	MC	1906	0604	97
Griggs, Chauncey L, Tacoma, Wash.	**W**	**1946**	**4604**	**19**
Guggenheim Museum, New York, NY.	E	1956	4305	
Hagan, Isaac Newton, Ohiopyle, Penn.	E	1954	4510	
Haldorn, Stuart, Carmel, California, site.	**W**	**1945**	**4502**	**38**
Hanna, Paul, Stanford, Calif.	**W**	**1937**	**3701**	**33**
Hanney & Sons, Evanston, Ill.	MC	1916	1506	38
Hardy, Thomas P, Racine, Wisc.	UGL	1905	0506	94
Harlan, Dr Allison, Chicago, Ill, site.	MC	1892	9204	
Harper, Ina Morris, St Joseph, Mich.	UGL	1959	5010	129
Hartford, Huntington Resort, Beverly Hills, site.	**W**	**1947**	**4721**	**51**
Hayashi, Aisaku, Tokyo, Japan.	**W**	**1917**	**1702**	**128**
Haynes, John, Fort Wayne, Ind.	E	1951	5110	
Heath, William R, Buffalo, NY.	E	1905	0507	
Hebert, AW, Evanston, Ill.	MC	1902	0112	40
Asbury Avenue.	MC	1902		41
Davis Street.	MC	1902		41
Heller, Isadore, Chicago, Ill.	MC	1896	9606	124
Henderson, FB, Elmhurst, Ill.	MC	1901	0104	102

Heurtley, Arthur, Oak Park, Ill.	MC	1902	0204	70
Cottage, Marquette Island, Mich.	UGL	1902	0214	98
Hickox, Warren, Kankakee, Ill.	E	1900	0004	
Hills, Edward R, Oak Park, Ill.	MC	1906	0102	69
Hillside Home School, Taliesin, Spring Green, Wisc.	UGL	1902	0216	46
Hoffman, Max, Rye, New York, NY.	E	1955	5535	
Hoffman Showroom, New York, NY.	E	1956	5622	
Hollyhock House – see Barnsdall, Aline.	**W**	**1917**	**1705**	**56**
Home and Studio, Oak Park, Ill – see Wright, Frank Lloyd.	MC	1889	8901	63
Honeycomb House – see Hanna, Paul.	**W**	**1937**	**3701**	**33**
Horner, LK, Chicago, Ill, site.	MC	1908	0807	113
Horse Show Association Fountain, Oak Park, Ill.	MC	1908	0305	77
Horshoe Inn, Estes Park, Colo, site.	**W**	**1908**	**0814**	**87**
House on the Mesa, Denver, Co, site.	**W**	**1931**	**3102**	**87**
Hoyt, PD, Geneva, Ill.	MC	1906	0605	95
Hughes, J Willis, Jackson, Miss.	E	1949	4908	
Humphreys Theater, Dallas, Texas.	**W**	**1955**	**5514**	**98**
Hunt, Stephen MB, La Grange, Ill.	MC	1907	0705	106
Hunt, Stephen MB, Oshkosh, Wisc.	UGL	1917	1703	35
Huntington Hartford Resort, Beverly Hills, Calif, site.	**W**	**1947**	**4721**	**51**
Husser, Joseph, Chicago, site.	MC	1899	9901	114
Hyde, H Howard, Chicago, Ill.	MC	1917	1506	130
Iber, Frank, Plover, Wisc.	UGL	1957	5518	34
Imperial Hotel, Tokyo, Japan, site.	**W**	**1915**	**1509**	**129**
Imperial Hotel Reconstruction, Inuyama City, Japan.	**W**	**1976**	**1509**	**130**
Ingalls, J Kibben, River Forest, Ill.	MC	1909	0906	56
Inoue, Viscount, Tokyo, Japan, site.	**W**	**1918**	**1804**	**132**
Irving, Edward P, Decatur, Ill.	E	1910	1003	
Jackson, Arnold, Beaver Dam, formerly Madison, Wisc.	UGL	1957	5518	67
Jacobs, Herbert, I, Madison, Wisc.	UGL	1936	3702	56
Jacobs, Herbert, II, Middleton, Wisc.	UGL	1948	4812	54
Jiyu Gakuen School of the Free Spirit, Tokyo, Japan.	**W**	**1921**	**2101**	**127**
Johnson, AP, Delavan, Wisc.	UGL	1905	0508	74
Johnson Desert Compound, Death Valley, Calif, site.	**W**	**1921**	**2306**	**41**
Johnson, Herbert F, Wingspread, Wind Point, Wisc.	UGL	1937	3703	88
Johnson, Oscar, see Hanney & Son, Evanston, Ill.	MC	1917	1506	38

Johnson Wax Company, Racine, Wisc.	UGL	1936	3601	91
Jones, Fred B, Delavan, Wisc.	UGL	1900	0103	72
Gatehouse.	UGL	1900	0103	71
Jones, Richard Lloyd, Tulsa, Okla.	**W**	**1929**	**2902**	**94**
Juvenile Cultural Center, Wichita, Kansas.	**W**	**1957**	**5743**	**90**
Kalil, Toufik, Manchester, NH.	E	1955	5506	
Kansas City Community Christian Church, Mo.	**W**	**1940**	**4004**	**118**
Kaufmann, Edgar, Fallingwater, Mill Run, Penn.	E	1936	3602	
Kaufmann, Edgar J, Palm Springs, Calif, site.	**W**	**1951**	**5111**	**43**
Kaufmann Office, now London, England.	E	1937	3704	
Keland, Willard H, Racine, Wisc.	UGL	1954	5417	90
Keys, Thomas E, Rochester, Minn.	UGL	1950	5012	28
Kier, William F, Ravine Bluffs (Lot 15), Glencoe, Ill.	MC	1915	1516	28
Kinney, Patrick, Lancaster, Wisc.	UGL	1951	5038	38
Kinney, Sterling, Amarillo, Texas.	**W**	**1957**	**5717**	**95**
Kissam, Daniel E, Ravine Bluffs (Lot 17), Glencoe, Ill.	MC	1915	1516	31
Kraus, Russell, Kirkwood, Mo.	**W**	**1951**	**5123**	**120**
Kundert Medical Clinic, San Luis Obispo, Calif.	**W**	**1956**	**5614**	**42**
Lacy, Rogers, Hotel, Dallas, Texas, site.	**W**	**1946**	**4606**	**99**
LaFond, Dr Edward, St Joseph, Minn.	UGL	1960	5518	20
Lake Delavan Yacht Club, Delavan, Wisc, site.	UGL	1902	0217	68
Lake Geneva Hotel, Lake Geneva, Wisc, site.	UGL	1912	1202	68
Lake Tahoe Summer Colony, Calif, site.	**W**	**1922**	**2205**	**38**
Lamberson, Jack, Oskaloosa, Iowa.	**W**	**1948**	**4712**	**114**
La Miniatura, Millard, Alice, Pasadena, Calif.	**W**	**1923**	**2302**	**61**
Lamp, Robert M, Madison, Wisc.	UGL	1903	0402	59
Lamp, Robert M, Rockyroost, Madison, Wisc, site.	UGL	1893	9301	58
Larkin Building, Buffalo, NY, site.	E	1903	0403	
Laurent, Kenneth, Rockford, Ill.	UGL	1949	4814	135
Laurent, Kenneth, Rockford, Ill.	MC	1949	4814	43
Lawrence Memorial Library, Springfield, Ill.	E	1905	0509	
Lenkurt Electric, San Mateo, California, site.	**W**	**1955**	**5520**	**31**
Levin, Robert, Kalamazoo, Mich.	UGL	1949	4911	125
Lewis, George, Talahassee, Fla.	E	1952	5207	
Lewis, Lloyd, Libertyville, Ill.	MC	1940	4008	17
Lincoln Center (Abraham), Chicago, Ill.	MC	1903	0010	120

Lindholm, RW, Cloquet, Minn.	UGL	1952	5208	19
Lindholm, Service Station, Cloquet, Minn.	UGL	1957	5739	18
Little, Francis W, Peoria, Ill.	E	1902	0009	
Living-room, Metropolitan Museum of Art, NY, NY.	E	1982	1304	
Original site, Deephaven, Minn.	UGL	1913	1304	137
Library, Allentown Museum of Art, Penn.	E	1988	1304	
Little Dipper, Barnsdall Park, Los Angeles, Calif.	**W**	**1921**	**2301**	**60**
Lockridge Medical Clinic, Whitefish, Montana.	**W**	**1958**	**5813**	**64**
Lovness, Donald, House, Stillwater, Minn.	UGL	1955	5507	24
Lovness, Donald, Cottage, Stillwater, Minn.	UGL	1955	5824	25
Lykes, Norman, Phoenix, Ariz.	**W**	**1966**	**5908**	**79**
MacHarg, William, Chicago, Ill, site.	MC	1891	9002	114
Manson, Charles L, Wausau, Wisc.	UGL	1940	4009	32
Marcus, Harold, Housing, Dallas, Texas, site.	**W**	**1935**	**3505**	**99**
Marcus, Stanley, Dallas, Texas, site.	**W**	**1935**	**3501**	**99**
Marden, Louis, McLean, Va.	E	1952	5220	
Marin County Civic Center, San Rafael, Calif.	**W**	**1957**	**5746**	**25**
Martin, Darwin D, Buffalo, NY.	E	1904	0405	
Martin, DD, Gardener's Cottage, Buffalo, NY.	E	1905	0530	
Martin, DD, Graycliff, Derby, New York, NY.	E	1927	2701	
Martin, William E, Oak Park, Ill.	MC	1902	0304	82
Mathews, Arthur C, Atherton, Calif.	**W**	**1950**	**5013**	**31**
May, Meyer, Grand Rapids, Mich.	UGL	1908	0817	105
McArthur, Warren, Chicago, Ill.	MC	1892	9205	122
McBean, James B, Rochester, Minn.	UGL	1957	5706	27
McCartney, Ward, Kalamazoo, Mich.	UGL	1949	4912	128
McCormick, Harold, Lake Forest, Ill, site.	MC	1907	0713	19
Meier, Delbert W, Monona, Iowa.	**W**	**1917**	**1506**	**107**
Meiji-mura Museum, Imperial Hotel Reconstruction, Inuyama City, Nagoya, Japan.	**W**	**1976**		**130**
Mendota Boathouse, Madison, Wisc.	UGL	1893	9304	58
Meteor Crater Inn, Winslow, Ariz, site.	**W**	**1948**	**4822**	**71**
Metropolitan Museum of Art, Little House, living room, New York City, NY.	E	1912	1304	
Meyer, Curtis, Galesburg, Mich.	UGL	1950	5015	122
Meyers Medical Clinic, Dayton, Ohio.	E	1956	5613	

Midway Gardens, Chicago, Ill, site.	MC	1914	1401	126
Mihara, Tokyo, Japan, site.	**W**	**1918**	**1807**	**132**
Millard, George Madison, Highland Park, Ill.	MC	1906	0606	22
Millard, Alice, Pasadena, Calif.	**W**	**1923**	**2302**	**61**
Miller, Alvin, Charles City, Iowa.	**W**	**1946**	**5016**	**106**
Miller, Arthur and Marilyn Monroe, site.	E	1957	5719	
Moe, Ingwald, Gary, Ind.	MC	1908	0531	110
Mollica, Joseph, Bayside, Wisc.	UGL	1958	5518	77
Moore, Nathan G, Oak Park, Ill.	MC	1895	9503	68
Monona Terrace, Madison, site.	UGL	1938	3909	58
Monroe, Marilyn and Arthur Miller, site.	E	1957	5719	
Mori Art Shop, Chicago, Ill, site.	MC	1914	1402	134
Morris Gift Shop, San Francisco, Calif.	**W**	**1948**	**4824**	**28**
Mossberg, Herman T, South Bend, Ind.	E	1949	4914	
Motion Picture Theater, Barnsdall Park, L. A., Calif, site.	**W**	**1920**	**2007**	**60**
Muirhead, Robert, Plato Center, Ill.	MC	1950	5019	45
Municipal Boathouse, Madison, Wisc, site.	UGL	1893	9308	58
Munkwitz Duplex, Milwaukee, Wisc, site.	UGL	1916	1606	79
Nakoma Country Club, Madison, Wisc, site.	UGL	1924	2403	52
Neils, Henry J, Minneapolis, Minn.	UGL	1950	5020	22
Nesbitt, John, Carmel, California, site.	**W**	**1940**	**4017**	**38**
Nicholas, Frederick D, Flossmoor, Ill.	MC	1906	0607	108
Noble, Elizabeth, Apartments, Los Angeles, site.	**W**	**1929**	**2903**	**51**
Northome, Little House, site.	UGL	1912	1304	137
Little House, library, Allentown, Penn.	E	1912	1304	
Little House, living room, New York City, NY.	E	1912	1304	
Oboler, Arch, Gatehouse, Malibu, Calif.	**W**	**1941**	**4112**	**48**
Ocotillo Camp, Chandler, Ariz, site.	**W**	**1928**	**2702**	**83**
O'Connor, JJ, Wilmette, Ill.	MC	1916	1506	37
Odawara Hotel, Kanagawa, Japan, site.	**W**	**1917**	**1706**	**133**
Olfelt, Paul, St Louis Park, Minn.	UGL	1958	5820	21
Olive Hill.				
Little Dipper, site.	**W**	**1923**	**2301**	**60**
Motion Picture Theater, site.	**W**	**1920**	**2007**	**60**
Studio Residence A.	**W**	**1920**	**2002**	**59**
Schemes for Olive Hill, site.	**W**	**1920**	**2005**	**60**

Studio Residence B, site.	**W**	**1920**	**2003**	**59**
Palmer, William, Ann Arbor, Mich.	**UGL**	**1950**	**5021**	**118**
Pappas, Theodore A, St Louis, Mo.	**W**	**1955**	**5516**	**119**
Park Ridge Country Club, Park Ridge, Ill, site.	MC	1912	1204	48
Parker, Robert P, Oak Park, Ill.	MC	1892	9206	62
Parkwyn Village, Kalamazoo, Mich.	UGL	1948	4806	124
Pauson, Rose, Phoenix, Ariz, site.	**W**	**1940**	**4011**	**78**
Pearce, Wilbur, Bradbury, Calif.	**W**	**1951**	**5114**	**62**
Pebbles & Balch shop, Oak Park, Ill, site.	MC	1907	0708	59
Pence, Martin, Hilo, Hawaii, site.	**W**	**1940**	**4019**	**121**
Penfield, Louis, Willoughby Hills, Ohio.	E	1953	5303	
Perry, Charles R, Ravine Bluffs, Glencoe, Ill.	MC	1915	1516	27
Peterson, Seth, Lake Delton, Wisc.	UGL	1958	5821	37
Pettit Memorial Chapel, Belvidere, Ill.	MC	1906	0619	44
Pew, John C, Shorewood Hills, Wisc.	UGL	1940	4012	64
Pfeiffer, Arthur, Taliesin West, Scottsdale, Ariz.	**W**	**1938**	**3807**	**86**
Pieper, Arthur, Paradise Valley, Phoenix, Ariz.	**W**	**1952**	**5218**	**82**
Pilgrim Congregational Church, Redding, Calif.	**W**	**1959**	**5818**	**22**
Pitkin, EH, Desbarats, Ontario, Canada.	UGL	1900	0005	96
Plaza Hotel Apartment, FLW, New York City, NY.	E	1955	5532	
Pope-Leighy House, Woodlawn, Virginia.	E	1940	4013	
Porter, Andrew T, Spring Green, Wisc.	UGL	1907	0709	48
Post Office, Marin County, Calif.	**W**	**1957**	**5746**	**26**
Post, Frederick B, Al Borah, Barrington Hills, Ill.	MC	1957	5518	47
Pratt, Eric, Galesburg, Mich.	UGL	1948	4827	120
Price, Harold Jr, Bartlesville, Okla.	**W**	**1954**	**5421**	**93**
Price, Harold, Sr, Paradise Valley, Phoenix, Ariz.	**W**	**1954**	**5419**	**81**
Price Tower, Bartlesville, Okla.	**W**	**1952**	**5215**	**92**
Ras El Bar, Egypt, site.	E	1927	7211	
Ravine Bluffs Development, Glencoe, Ill.	MC	1915	1516	25
Ravine Bluffs Housing,				
Lot 10: Perry, Charles R.	MC	1915	1516	27
Lot 15: Ellis, CJ.	MC	1915	1516	29
Lot 16: Finch, Frank B.	MC	1915	1516	30
Lot 17: Compton, JM.	MC	1915	1516	31
Lot 22: Gilfillan, SJ.	MC	1915	1516	28

Rayward, John L, New Canaan, Conn.	E	1955	5523	
Rebhuhn, Ben, Great Neck Estates, NY.	E	1937	3801	
Reisley, Roland, Pleasantville, NY.	E	1951	5115	
Richards Co of Milwaukee see American Systems Bungalow.				
Richardson, Stuart, Glen Ridge, NJ.	E	1941	4104	
River Forest Golf Club, Ill, site.	MC	1898	9802	59
River Forest Tennis Club, Ill.	MC	1906	0510	`58
Riverview Terrace Restaurant, Spring Green, Wisc.	UGL	1956	5619	45
Roberts, Abby Beecher, Marquette, Mich.	UGL	1936	3603	97
Roberts, Charles E, Oak Park, Ill.	MC	1896	9603	87
Roberts, Isabel, River Forest, Ill.	MC	1908	0808	55
Robie, Frederick C, Chicago, Ill.	MC	1909	0908	125
Rockyroost, Lamp, Robert M, Madison, site.	UGL	1893	9301	58
Roloson, Robert W, Row Houses, Chicago, Ill.	MC	1894	9404	119
Romeo and Juliet Windmill, Spring Green, Wisc.	UGL	1896	9607	49
Rookery Building Lobby, Chicago, Ill.	MC	1905	0511	135
Root, Hollis R, Ravine Bluffs (Lot 22), Glencoe, Ill.	MC	1916	1605	29
Rosenbaum, Florence, Ala.	E	1939	3903	
Ross, Charles S, Delavan, Wisc.	UGL	1902	0206	70
Ross, William W, Ravine Bluffs (Lot 16), Glencoe, Ill.	MC	1915	1516	30
Roux Library, Florida Southern College, Lakeland, Fla.	E	1941	3805	
Rubin, Nathan, Canton, Ohio.	E	1951	5116	
Rudin, Walter, Madison, Wisc.	UGL	1957	5706	61
St Marks in the Bowerie, New York City, NY, site.	E	1929	2905	
San Antonio Transit Admin. Building, Texas, site.	**W**	**1946**	**4725**	**101**
San Diego, Cinema, Calif, site.	**W**	**1905**	**0517**	**43**
San Francisco Bay Bridge, Calif, site.	**W**	**1949**	**4921**	**29**
San Francisco Call Building, Calif, site.	**W**	**1912**	**1207**	**29**
San Marcos in the Desert, Chandler, Ariz, site.	**W**	**1928**	**2704**	**83**
Sander, Frank S, Stamford, Conn.	E	1953	5304	
Sarabhai Calico Mill Store, Ahmedabad, India, site	**W**	**1945**	**4508**	**136**
Schaberg, Donald, Okemos, Mich.	UGL	1950	5022	111
Schemes for Olive Hill, Barnsdall Park, L. A., Calif, site.	**W**	**1920**	**2005**	**60**
Schoolhouse, Crosbyton, Texas, site.	**W**	**1905**	**1008**	**101**
Schultz, Carl, St Joseph, Mich.	UGL	1957	5745	130
Schwartz, Bernard, Two Rivers, Wisc.	UGL	1939	3904	36

Scoville Park Fountain, Oak Park, Ill.	MC	1909	0305	77
Scully, Vincent, site.	E	1948	4816	
Serlin, Edward, Pleasantville, NY.	E	1949	4917	
Shavin, Seamour, Chattanooga, Tenn.	E	1950	5023	
Smith Bank, Dwight, Ill.	E	1905	0512	
Smith, George W, Oak Park, Ill.	MC	1896	9803	78
Smith, Melvin Maxwell, Bloomfield Hills, Mich.	UGL	1949	4818	116
Smith, Richard, Jefferson, Wisc.	UGL	1959	5026	65
Snowflake, Wall, Carlton D, Plymouth, Mich.	UGL	1941	4114	113
Sondern, Clarence, Kansas City, Mo.	**W**	**1940**	**4014**	**117**
Sottil, Helen, Curnevaca, Mexico, site.	**W**	**1957**	**5722**	**123**
Southwest Christian Seminary, Phoenix, Ariz.	**W**	**1950**	**5033**	**72**
Spencer, Dudley, Wilmington, Delaware.	E	1956	5605	
Spencer, George W, Delavan, Wisc.	UGL	1902	0207	69
Staley, Karl A, North Madison, Ohio.	E	1951	5119	
Steffens, Oscar, Chicago, Ill, site.	MC	1909	0909	113
Steinway Hall, Chicago, Ill, site.	MC	-	-	136
Stevens, C Leigh, Auldbrass Plantation, Yemassee, SC.	E	1940	4015	
Stewart, George C, Montecito, Calif.	**W**	**1909**	**0907**	**44**
Stockman, George C, Mason City, Iowa.	**W**	**1908**	**0809**	**105**
Stohr Arcade, Chicago, Ill, site.	MC	1909	0910	114
Storer, John, Hollywood, Los Angeles, Calif.	**W**	**1923**	**2304**	**53**
Stromquist, Donald, Bountiful, Utah.	**W**	**1958**	**5626**	**69**
Sturges, George D, Brentwood Heights, Calif.	**W**	**1939**	**3905**	**49**
Sullivan, Louis (Albert), Chicago, Ill, site.	MC	1892	9207	121
Sullivan, Louis, Ocean Springs, Miss.	E	1890	9003	
Sugarloaf Mountain, Strong, Maryland, site.	E	1924	2505	
Sunday, Robert H, Marshalltown, Iowa.	**W**	**1955**	**5522**	**111**
Suntop Homes, Ardmore, Penn.	E	1939	3906	
Sutton, Harvey P, McCook, Nebr.	**W**	**1907**	**0710**	**89**
Sweeton, JA, Cherry Hill, NJ.	E	1959	5027	
Taliesin, Spring Green, Wisc.	UGL	1911	1104	42
Taliesin West, Scottsdale, Ariz.	**W**	**1938**	**3803**	**85**
Tan-y-deri, Porter, Andrew D, Spring Green, Wisc.	UGL	1907	0709	48
Teater, Archie B, Bliss, Idaho.	**W**	**1952**	**5211**	**68**
Thaxton, William L, Bunker Hill, Houston, Texas.	**W**	**1954**	**5414**	**100**

Thomas, Frank W, Oak Park, Ill.	MC	1901	0106	73
Thurber Art Gallery, Chicago, Ill, site.	MC	1909	0911	134
Tirranna, Rayward, John, New Canaan, Conn.	E	1955	5523	
Todd A-O Theaters, Cinerama, Los Angeles, Calif, site.	**W**	**1958**	**5819**	**51**
Tomek, Ferdinand F, Riverside, Ill.	MC	1907	0711	90
Tonkens, Gerald B, Amberly Village, Ohio.	E	1955	5510	
Tracy, William B, Normandy Park, Wash.	**W**	**1954**	**5512**	**17**
Trier, Paul J, Johnston, Des Moines, Iowa.	**W**	**1957**	**5724**	**112**
Turkel, H, Detroit, Mich.	UGL	1955	5513	117
Unitarian Meeting House, Shorewood Hills, Wisc.	UGL	1947	5031	62
Unity Chapel, Spring Green, Wisc.	UGL	1886	8601	50
Unity Temple, Oak Park, Ill.	MC	1906	0611	75
Usonian Exhibition House, New York, NY.	E	1953	5314	
Usonia Homes, Pleasantville, NY.	E	1947	4720	
Vallarino, JJ , Panama City, Panama, site.	**W**	**1951**	**5113**	**123**
Valley National Bank, Ariz, sites,				
Sunnyslope.	**W**	**1948**	**4734**	**78**
Tucson.	**W**	**1947**	**4722**	**78**
Studio Residence A, Barnsdall Park, LA, Calif, site.	**W**	**1920**	**2002**	**59**
Residence B, Barnsdall Park, LA, Calif, site.	**W**	**1920**	**2003**	**59**
Vanderkloot, William J, Lake Bluff, Ill.	MC	1916	1506	18
Van Tamlen, Eugene, Madison, Wisc.	UGL	1956	5518	60
Vosburgh, Ernest, Grand Beach, Mich.	UGL	1916	1607	132
Walker, Mrs Clinton, Carmel, Calif.	**W**	**1951**	**5122**	**37**
Wall, Carlton D, Plymouth, Mich.	UGL	1941	4114	113
Waller Apartments, Chicago, Ill.	MC	1895	9504	118
Waller Bathing Pavilion, Charlevoix, Mich, site.	UGL	1909	0916	100
Waller, Edward C, River Forest, Ill, site.	MC	1899	9902	49
Wallis, Henry, Delavan, Wisc.	UGL	1900	0114	73
Walser, JJ, Chicago, Ill.	MC	1903	0306	116
Walter, Lowell, Quasqueton, Iowa.	**W**	**1945**	**4505**	**108**
Walton, Dr Robert G, Modesto, Calif.	**W**	**1957**	**5623**	**39**
Wedding Chapel, Claremont Hotel, Berkeley, Calif, site.	**W**	**1957**	**5709**	**29**
Weisblatt, David I, Galesburg, Mich.	UGL	1948	4918	123
Weltzheimer, Charles T, Oberlin, Ohio.	E	1948	4819	
Wenatchee Town Plan, Washington, site.	**W**	**1919**	**1904**	**19**

West Coast Office, San Francisco, Calif, site.	**W**	**1952**	**5226**	**29**
Western Pennsylvania Conservancy, Fallingwater.	E	1935	3602	
Westcott, Burton J, Springfield, Ohio.	E	1907	0712	
Westhope, Jones, Richard Lloyd, Tulsa, Okla.	**W**	**1929**	**2902**	**94**
White, William A, Emporia, Kansas, site.	**W**	**1916**	**1610**	**91**
Williams, Chauncey L, River Forest, Ill.	MC	1895	9505	54
Willey, Malcom E, Minneapolis, Minn.	UGL	1933	3401	23
Willits, Ward W, Highland Park, Ill.	MC	1901	0208	23
Wilson, Abraham, Millstone, NJ.	E	1954	5402	
Windfohr, Robert F, Fort Worth, Texas, site.	**W**	**1949**	**4919**	**101**
Winn, Robert D, Kalamazoo, Mich.	UGL	1948	4815	126
Winslow, William Herman, River Forest, Ill.	MC	1894	9305	52
Women's Building, Spring Green, Wisc, site.	UGL	1914	1413	40
Wooley, Francis J, Oak Park, Ill.	MC	1893	9405	67
World's Columbian Exhibition of 1893, Chicago.	MC	-	-	126
Wright, Anna, Oak Park, Ill.	MC	-	-	65
Wright, David, Phoenix, Ariz.	**W**	**1950**	**5030**	**80**
Wright, Duey, Wausau, Wisc.	UGL	1957	5727	33
Wright, Frank Lloyd,				
Apartment, Plaza, NY, site.	E	1954	5532	
Desert Compound, Mojave, Calif, site.	**W**	**1924**	**2107**	**41**
House and Studio, Oak Park, Ill.	MC	1889	8901	63
Office, Los Angeles, Calif, site.	**W**	**1922**	**-**	**52**
Studio, Chicago, Ill, sites.	MC	1911	1113	133
Studio, Los Angeles, Calif, site.	**W**	**1922**	**2201**	**51**
Wright, Robert Llewellyn, Bethesda, Maryland.	E	1953	5312	
Wynant, Wilber, Gary, Ind.	MC	1915	1506	109
Wyoming Valley Grammar School, Spring Green, Wisc.	UGL	1957	5741	51
Yahara Boat Club, Madison, Wisc, site.	UGL	1905	0211	58
Yamamura, Tazaemon, Ashiya, Hyogo, Japan.	**W**	**1918**	**1803**	**134**
Yosemite National Park Resturant, Calif, site.	**W**	**1954**	**5307**	**41**
Young, Harrison P, Oak Park, Ill.	MC	1895	9507	79
Young, Owen D, Chandler, Ariz, site.	**W**	**1927**	**2707**	**83**
Zaferiou, Socrates, Blauvelt, NY.	E	1961	5518	
Zeigler, Jessie R, Frankfort, Kent.	E	1910	1007	
Zimmerman, Isadore, Manchester, NH.	E	1952	5214	